Playing Piano in a Brothel

Memoirs of a film director

by Peter Duffell

Published in the USA by:
BearManor Media
P O Box 71426
Albany, Georgia 31708
www.bearmanormedia.com

Printed in the United States of America
ISBN 978-1-59393-612-9

Book and cover design and layout by Darlene Swanson • www.van-garde.com
Cover photograph by Rosslyn Cliffe Duffell.

When asked what he did for a living,
he replied, "I'm a film director,
but don't tell my mother - she thinks
I play piano in a brothel"

~

Variation on an old joke — probably a Jewish one,
because all the best jokes are Jewish, like many
of the most talented people in the film industry.

Contents:

For Rosslyn

Foreword

by Sir Christopher Lee

I am very pleased to do this foreword for Peter Duffell. In fact it's a privilege. I have known Peter for a long time, which rather dates us, but that's something you can't do anything about—anno domini.

People are inclined to forget, or simply not to know, that when a film appears in front of their eyes on the screen, on television or in the cinema it is basically, of course—although others are included—the work and total involvement of the director.

I think my first film with him was *The House That Dripped Blood*. I immediately liked him as a director because I knew that he knew what he was doing, which is sometimes far from being the case.

Then we went to India where we did *The Far Pavilions*. Now this was a tremendous challenge to everybody, but particularly to a director who had a very big cast—hundreds of extras, animals galore and castles and those sorts of things. To handle something of this size means you have to be really good at what you do—and in my opinion, Peter Duffell is the most under-rated director we have had in Britain for a very long time.

I think probably the most important thing between all of us when we make a film is respect. In other words, you trust the director. He acknowledges that he can help you or he can ignore you. Peter has always been very fine at the former. One can place complete trust in him. If your crew likes you it doesn't just mean that they think you're a good chap to get on with, it means they respect you—and if the cast likes you they will do their damnedest to deliver what is on the printed page, and above all to play scenes as the director wants them to do.

I am sure this book will be a great success and will help people to understand how films are made, particularly when the result is clearly the work of a highly skilled hand.

I wish you every success, Peter, and maybe we will make another film together one day!

—Christopher Lee

Acknowledgements

My thanks to Sir Christopher Lee who kindly wrote a foreword to this book. My thanks, too, for the happy and incomparable experience of working with him on two movies and his valued friendship over many years.

Many thanks to my friend Mark Miller who wrote so perceptibly about my Christopher Lee/Peter Cushing movie. His tireless support for my book and critical suggestions helped me tremendously.

Thank you to Ingrid Pitt for also writing a piece for me and for photographs of herself and Jon Pertwee in *The House That Dripped Blood,* which were missing from my own archives.

My gratitude to the late Graham Greene, whose approval of *England Made Me* made me a very proud film maker.

Also to…

Quentin Falk who wrote the excellent study of Graham Greene movies *Travels in Greeneland* and who supported me at numerous event showings of *England Made Me.*

The many film crews I have worked with over the years.

And the producers Joe Janni, Sydney Cole, Milton Subotsky, Judd Bernard and Buzz Berger.

Professor Eric Robinson, MA, of Jesus College Cambridge, who helped me get to Oxford University.

And last but far from least, my dear wife Rosslyn. Without her patience, tireless support and keen eye for detail and grammar, this book would probably not have been written.

Trailer

What does a film director actually do? In *La Nuit Americaine* (*Day for Night*), the best film ever made about the movie industry and the trials and tribulations of the director, François Truffaut, playing himself in the film, gives an ironic answer to the question. In a sequence where he is pursued by costume designers, property masters, set dressers and just about everybody involved in the picture, all demanding decisions from him, he says a film director is somebody who is supposed to have all the answers and doesn't always have them, but if he is to remain in control, he has got to look as though he has. The talented film director Michael Reeves, who died tragically young and is remembered only by horror movie buffs for his film *Witchfinder General* starring Vincent Price, once observed that everybody wants to be a film director but not everyone wants to learn how to direct.

Film buffs know the answer to the question, more or less, but many people who enjoy going to the cinema or watching movies on television have only the vaguest idea, often confusing the director with the producer of a film. The answer is both simple and complicated. Simply, whereas the producer, who may have initiated the project in the first place, is concerned with raising finance for the movie, getting a distribution deal, and dealing with all sorts of legal and contractual problems, the director actually <u>makes</u> the film. In order to do so, he has to deal with the whole complex of relationships and contributory talents that are necessary to the process of producing a movie.

The first stage will be cementing the relationship with the producer, who will have offered the assignment to him as he considers him to be the right man for the job. Then there will be a development process with the producer and the scriptwriter if the director is not writing the script himself. When the script is finally in a shape that everybody is happy with—and it may well have gone through a number of drafts and a great deal of argument, painful disagreement and moments of doubt and despair for the parties concerned—it will probably then have to be submitted to the final decision makers. These are the men in suits at the company that will distribute the film and who must give their approval. Later they will also expect to be consulted about the actors whom the producer and director propose to play the leading roles. Then, at this point, the film may actually get the "go ahead" and—miracle of miracles—move into production. Once on the studio floor, the director must really take command. He tells the actors what the film is about, and this means much more than a simple exposition of the plot and their characters. He must discuss how he sees their dramatic development during the story, and in each scene he must say where he would like them to move or even simply stand in the set. He has to indicate to them their positions in the picture composition and whether or not they are being filmed in close-up. All these details, some of them artistically important and some of them just tiresome and technical, will be important and helpful to them in giving a good performance. With the cinematographer, he will discuss the lighting style of the film, and with the camera-operator the camera movement and the composition of the image that he has in mind. He should also know something about the choice of lenses for any sequence of his film. He will have been asked to approve the wardrobe with the costume designer, and he will also have conferred with the production designer about the sets and the outdoor locations.

When the filming is completed and the end-of-picture party over (with all the emotional goodbyes, sincere or otherwise), then the director spends weeks in the cutting rooms working with the editor to put all the shots together in the most effective way. This can be a period of gloom, uncertainty and self-criticism at not having got the best out of the performers or having shot the material clumsily and not picked up the shot that his better judgement had told him he needed, even though the producer was wringing his hands in fear of going over schedule.

The relationship between a director and his crew really comes down to how much they respect him. With a director who doesn't know what he's doing and who is unsure of himself, a film crew can be quite ruthless, but if he earns their respect—and the word *earn* is important—then they will support him all the way. The making of a film is in many ways a team effort, but in the end the director is the creative force behind it; if the film has any pretensions towards making any sort of artistic statement, then it is his vision that is realised for good or bad. The Russian director Tarkovsky once said in an interview that if a film is a failure, then it is the director who gets the blame; on the other hand, if the film is a success, then everybody wants to get credit for it. I don't know if he was bitter or just wryly ironic, but more than a grain of truth lies in his witticism.

Much of getting to direct is pure luck, and getting to direct a commercially successful movie is a question of even greater luck. You can make an artistically good film, but if it doesn't do well at the box office, your career can come to a staggering halt. Different people get there in different ways but once you get there you have to prove that you can actually do it.

When people at parties ask what you do for a living and you unwisely tell them, then they ask what films you have made that they may have seen. Reluctantly, you throw off a few titles, usually the ones of which you are most proud, to be rewarded with an embarrassed shake of the head and an admission that said titles mean nothing to your interrogator. They have, of course, seen all the *Star Wars* movies, the James Bond actioners and Ridley Scott's mega-budget blockbusters, as well as *Harry Potter* and *Lord of the Rings*, but your serious work that went out on BBC television or possibly played in the art houses, alas, has passed them by.

The other question you often get asked, particularly by serious young men and women who want to get into the industry, is how did you become a movie director. The flip answer is "Luck, I guess," followed by the piano in a brothel joke, but the serious answer (and the polite one) is "I will tell you how I did it, but there is no standard answer. Everybody's story is different, and I don't think my story will be any great help or guideline for you, although I hope you may find it interesting."

Will you take us in please?

This is not really an autobiography, but a memoir about how I became a film director, so I will not bore you with long opening chapters about my personal history, and I will be as brief as possible in that area.

I was born in the so-called "Dickens Inn" —the Sun Hotel in Canterbury that my grandmother owned at the time. Family legend had that it was, in fact, the room where Mr. Micawber in *David Copperfield* looked out of the window, waiting for "something to turn up." Mr. Micawber's hopefulness was perhaps a harbinger of my future in the movie industry.

As a result of my parents' broken marriage, I had a fairly chaotic early childhood. I was sent to a series of different "educational establishments" even including two convent schools, for, in those days, Catholic nuns were commonly held to be excellent teachers. Then I was a pupil for a short time at a small private boarding school of the kind found in the pages of Evelyn Waugh. It was called, rather pretentiously, The South West London College, where, as I later discovered from a paperback biography bought at Heathrow Airport, Errol Flynn had been a pupil for a time. Later I went to Upper Latymer School in Hammersmith, London, where, a generation or two before me, Louis Hayward, the Hollywood star of the thirties, had been a pupil and, a generation or two after me, there was Hugh Grant, but none of this had anything to do with my eventual arrival behind a movie camera. I did, however, have an early love of the cinema. I and my friend Donald Morley, who sat behind me in class, used to trick our way into adult-rated movies either by lying about our age, which was seldom successful, or by asking somebody to "take us in please," which usually worked. This way we managed to see classics of the horror genre such as Bela Lugosi in *Dracula* and Boris Karloff's extraordinarily poignant performance as *Frankenstein*'s monster. We enjoyed being scared in the safety of our cinema seats, secure in the knowledge that even the most terrifying monsters that erupted from the screen were made real only by our "suspension of disbelief."

We were also great addicts of the Warner Bros. movies that starred actors like Edward G. Robinson, James Cagney and the great Humphrey Bogart, and we vied with each other in esoteric movie buff knowledge. Who played the police chief in Eric Ambler's *Mask of Demetrius*? What was the name of the Alan Jenkins character in *Dead End*? And what role did John Abbott play in such and such a movie? But it did not seem possible to me that I could ever enter that magic world of film making. No obvious

Film poster for *The Mummy's Ghost*
starring Lon Chaney and Ramsay Ames.

windows of opportunity existed to climb through when I was young, which may seem strange today when film schools abound and opportunities for bright young people to enter the industry are there for all to take.

We were heavily involved in the school drama group, and Donald entered the acting profession after we left school. I remember a production of R.C.Sherriff's play about the First World War, *Journey's End*, which I directed and in which I had the presumption to cast myself as Stanhope, the tortured commanding officer; Donald played Osborne, the middle-aged officer whom the others called Uncle. We particularly enjoyed doing the play because it meant that we could use the word "bloody" on the stage, and that, in my school-days, was pretty strong language, the "f" word not having then passed into common parlance. Like all grammar schools of the time, we had a Cadet Corps with khaki uniforms that we were able to borrow for the production. Interestingly, they were called *Cadet Corps* and not OTC (*Officers Training Corps*) which was what similar organisations were called in public schools like Eton and Harrow. Sifting through their equipment, I came across a dummy artillery shell. It gave me the bright idea that at the end of the play, when the dugout was supposed to collapse under enemy bombardment, it would be great to throw said dummy shell onto the stage. Unfortunately, the chap assigned to do it, in a moment of zeal, lobbed it on stage before the enemy attack began, so several schoolboy Thespians, ignoring the sniggers from the audience, had to carry on with the dialogue pretending that it had not happened. I also played Charles Dickens' Scrooge-like employer in a one-act play about his youth called *The Dickens of Gray's Inn*. A little later, I trod the boards again in a local amateur production of Shaw's *Major Barbara*, in which I played Adolphus Cousins. Ours was a left-wing group operating under the banner of London's Unity Theatre, but it manifested all the internal jealousies and petty squabbling which are probably to be found in any amateur theatrical enterprise. It resulted in a visit from Oscar Lewenstein, at that time a sort of political commissar at Unity—he later became an important figure at the Royal Court Theatre—who lectured us on this unacceptably bourgeois behaviour. Some time later I concluded that I was no great shakes as an actor, but at least I learnt something of what it is like to be in front of an audience or on a film set in front of the camera.

After leaving school, I had a false start in the electronics industry where, despite having obtained relevant academic qualifications, I felt that I did not really belong. I lived at this time in a room at the top of a large house in Well Walk, Hampstead. It belonged to a professor of music at the Royal College named Alfred Nieman. On the lower floor lived William Glock, the distinguished music critic, later Director of Music at the BBC, and his wife Clement, who was the Head of the Scene Painting Department at the Royal Opera House and for whom my girlfriend Patricia worked. I was very young and deeply impressed by the group of writers and musicians who revolved around the Glock household, among them people like the music critic John Amis and the famous Amadeus Quartet. Sometimes on summer evenings, we would play softball cricket on Hampstead Heath and then return to William's flat where, on one magical occasion, he and Norbert Brainin, the first violin of the Quartet, played Beethoven's *Spring Sonata*. I am eternally grateful to William for opening my ears to a great deal of wonderful music of which I was then totally ignorant. This was, of course, in the pre-vinyl days of the seventy-eight record. William had a splendid wind-up EMG gramophone with thorn needles to minimise the damage to the wax record. It had a graceful acoustic horn that gave the best reproduction possible if one did not have an electronic amplifier system. William played classic recordings of the Mozart piano concertos by Edwin Fischer and introduced me to the astonishing beauty of Nadia Boulanger's recordings of the Renaissance genius Monteverdi. A passion for these two composers has remained with me.

Because Patricia worked at the Opera House, I was able to see many operas and ballets for free. I often sat in the electricians' perch in the wings from where I saw famous visiting ballet stars of the time. In one memorable performance of *Die Valkure*, the great baritone Hans Hotter was giving his Wotan when he fell dramatically behind the scenery as he ascended the funeral pyre of Brunhilde (sung in that production by Kirsten Flagstad). Fortunately, he was not hurt and, after climbing back onto the rocks, continued as though nothing untoward had happened. In true British sporting fashion, he got an extra long ovation at the final curtain. I was also lucky enough to watch great conductors like Sir Thomas Beecham in rehearsal. A wonderful dress rehearsal of *Die Meistersinger* that he conducted had a memorable Beecham moment. During the prize song scene, the chorus marched on stage carrying the banners of the competing Guilds, and it was a splendid visual moment in the production. Suddenly Sir Thomas tapped his rostrum and the orchestra and everybody else fell silent. One could almost feel the trepidation of the musicians and the singers. What was wrong? Who had played or sung a wrong note? On whose head would fall the fearful wrath of the maestro? The silence was held agonisingly for several seconds, which must have seemed like a lifetime to the artists. Then—"I'm going for a pee," said the great man, and he disappeared down into the depths behind the orchestra pit. Nobody dared laugh, but the relief was evident both in the auditorium and presumably the backstage toilets.

I have had a great love of jazz from my adolescence and for a time ran a jazz aficionados' club with Max Jones, who later became jazz correspondent for the musical journal *The Melody Maker,* and wrote, in collaboration with the trumpeter John Chilton, a highly respected book on Louis Armstrong. In those first years after the War, a musicians' union embargo was enacted on American musicians coming to England to work, but when that was lifted, we were able to hear for the first time many of our idols who came over to give live performances. Besides Louis, of course, came the divine Billie Holiday, Duke Ellington and so many others. I remember a wonderful Ellington concert at the London Hammersmith Odeon and their spine-tingling performance of that old Duke classic, *Rockin' in Rhythm.* Max, as a professional journalist, got to know all of them, and at his house at various parties given in their honour, I met stars like Josh White, Big Bill Broonzy and Cab Calloway, who came to London to play Sportin' Life in *Porgy and Bess.*

I was also lucky enough, in my youth, to go to the New Theatre in St. Martin's Lane to see such famous performances as Ralph Richardson's *Peer Gynt* and Falstaff and Olivier's extraordinary *Richard III,* which he later filmed along with his *Hamlet.* While I lived in Hampstead, there was a Donald Wolfit season of Shakespeare at an old theatre in Camden Town where we saw his astonishing *King Lear* for the first time. Wolfit's repertory company was notoriously tatty, often with indifferent actors in supporting roles, cheap, old-fashioned scenery and musty costumes, but his Lear was recognised even by his most acidic critics as one of the great performances of the time. The legend had it that on the nights when he was giving his Lear, he felt something extraordinary happen to him as he walked through the stage door. Watching him come on stage at the beginning of the play, when the old king splits up his kingdom between his nasty daughters and their husbands, one wondered how he could sustain such extraordinary energy throughout the evening, but he always did, and his descent into madness and the death of Cordelia was almost unbearably moving. He would always come on stage again after the play was over, hang on the curtain dramatically exhausted, and offer a little prayer to the Master Dramatist whose humble servant he was.

After attending a series of extramural evening lectures at King's College London, I wrote a paper on Chaucer's poem *Troilus and Criseyde* and managed to get a Government scholarship for a university course. With the help of my tutor, Eric Robinson, I got a place at Keble College Oxford to read English Literature. So I chucked up my job in electronics and the direction of my life changed completely.

Although to many of my friends (even those who had been in the Services), a place at University was a natural and expected thing, for me it had been beyond my wildest dreams. Cycling over Magdalen Bridge to tutorials and lectures felt like Heaven. Oxford at this time was an exciting place to be. To come up for the first time to find one's mailbox full of invitations to join clubs of all descriptions, from debating societies and philosophical discussion groups to the Oxford Dramatic Society (OUDS) and the Union, was somehow to acquire a new identity. Ken Tynan had gone down in a blaze of glory, and his undergraduate production of the *First Quarto Hamlet* was still being talked about. The previous year had seen Nevill Coghill's production of *The Tempest* in the gardens of Worcester College, long remembered for its spectacular closing scene in which Ariel, having been given his marching orders by Prospero, runs off across the lake where a wooden platform had been built just under the surface of the water.

Early in my first term I lunched in the OUDS clubroom, pretending to be absorbed in my copy of *The New Statesman* and not the least bit impressed by the people sitting at the next table: John Schlesinger, Tony Richardson and Michael Codron, among others who were now in their second or third years and whose stars were well in the ascendant. I, too, was active in student theatre and became a committee member of the Experimental Theatre Club. I produced and acted in the college play in my first year: Bernard Shaw's absurdist comedy *Too True To Be Good*. The play opens in the bedroom of the leading lady who is suffering from some minor ailment. Beside the bed is a microbe who complains that the tiresome woman has made him ill! A typical piece of Shavian nonsense in which he inverts received ideas and so questions their validity. The microbe was played in outrageous high camp style by Clement Crisp, who went on to become one of the most distinguished ballet critics, writing for The Financial Times. I had the nerve, or the arrogance, to cast myself as Aubrey, the Oxford-educated burglar who drives the play along and who harangues the audiences with an enormous speech at the end of the last act.

The custom for the dramatic society was to ask an old member of the College who had become a professional actor to come up to give a little advice on the production. Leslie Banks, who starred in Laurence Olivier's film of Shakespeare's *Henry V*, was a Keble man and in the thirties presented the college dramatic society with a collapsible stage construction that could be erected in College Hall. During the war, however, the College Bursar had it broken up and used for blackout purposes. This did not endear him to Leslie Banks, so it would not have been politic to approach him. However, Michael Goodliffe, another distinguished Keble thespian, came up to have a look at my offering. Michael was kindness itself, but I was painfully aware of how much I had to learn about acting and directing. I did work with him once, in later years, and was saddened to hear that he died in tragic circumstances.

I wrote on theatre and cinema for the University magazines *Isis* and *Cherwell*. When Josh White came to do a concert, I wrote a profile of him for the *Isis* and threw a party for him after the show. Josh was more than happy to play and sing to us and enjoy the adulation of the students who were lucky enough to be there.

We invited Peter Ustinov to come down and talk to members of the Experimental Theatre Club. He graciously accepted, and one sunny evening in the Spring Term, we committee members stood on Broad Street outside Exeter College where the event was to be held, anxiously awaiting the arrival of the great man. Looking interestingly dishevelled, he turned up in a vast open sports car. The evening proved a real success. Ustinov spoke at great length, without any notes, about the theatre, the actors' art and his own distinguished career. I can no longer remember what he actually said but he was, as always, witty and entertaining. We had booked him a room at the Randolph Hotel, and after the meeting, the committee members, feeling privileged and important, went back with him and sat for a long time in the hotel lounge while he regaled us with a series of hilarious and wicked anecdotes about his fellow thespians, enlivened by his brilliant mimicry of John Gielgud, J.B. Priestley and other famous persons whom he knew and loved, for there was not a hint of malice in any of his stories.

The University Jazz Club thrived, and on one memorable evening we had Mick Mulligan's band with the singer George Melly as our guests. In response to a highly appreciative undergraduate audience, Mick and the group played on after the time at which the University decreed all frivolous student activities should be over and everybody back in college or their lodgings. This resulted in a visit from the University proctors squad who patrolled the streets of Oxford every night looking for delinquent male undergraduates, perhaps climbing over the walls of the ladies' colleges or even trying to climb back into their own colleges after the doors were locked for the night. They must have heard the sounds of New Orleans resounding around Walton Street, I think, but they certainly didn't turn up because of a love of the music; the unfortunate result of their visit was that the club lost its permission to function for quite a while after that. Many years later I reminded George Melly of the incident: he laughed and said that Mick saw the proctors come in with the blue-suited college porters who always backed them up. "Who are the c...s in bowler hats?" asked Mick in a loud voice, and that probably had more to do with the closure of the club than anything else.

One of my best friends at Oxford was the poet and writer, Martin Seymour Smith. Martin was a friend of the great Robert Graves and passionate about Graves' poetry, which deeply influenced his own work. Thanks to Martin, I got a job during the following summer vacation as a live-in tutor and general nanny to Simon Gough, the ten-year old son of Graves' niece, the actress Diana Graves who was appearing with Peter Ustinov in his play, *The Love of Four Colonels*. It was the year of the Festival of Britain, and one afternoon, at Diana's suggestion, I took a reluctant young Simon to the South Bank to look at the various sculptures on display there. He was bored and sulky, but on the way home I said that I felt he should tell a little white lie and say to his mother that he had really enjoyed himself. To my relief, he dutifully did so, but payback time had to come. A few days later, I discovered that he had somehow acquired a rather wicked-looking pocket knife that I felt was too dangerous for a ten-year old. When I decided to confiscate it he remonstrated, saying that he had done me a favour by lying to his mother about the Festival of Britain trip, so why couldn't I do him a favour, too, and let him keep it. I said, "No way," but the least I could do was not to tell his Mum about it. Later, Simon followed his mother and his father, Michael Gough, into the acting profession.

One afternoon, while Diana was playing *bezique*— a card game fashionable at the time—with her friends, Stanley Baker, his wife Elizabeth and another actor named David Oxley, Peter Ustinov turned up having just come from a car race meeting at Silverstone. When he came through the door, it was as though he had brought with him a whole group of excitable Italian mechanics from the Ferrari pits, and he kept us in fits of laughter. One could almost hear the cars and smell the oil and petrol fumes. I met Peter Ustinov once or twice after that at various film festivals, but I never had the privilege of working with him

Of course, there was also a degree to be taken at the end of three years. That meant the weekly essay and tutorial, sitting in the Radcliffe Camera which housed the English library, trying to concentrate on a certain amount of serious reading and not being distracted by the more attractive female undergraduates. I attended lectures by awe-inspiring literary scholars such as C.S.Lewis and J.R.R.Tolkien, whose lectures on the poem *Sir Gawain and the Green Knight* had to be attended if one hoped to make any kind of a stab at the examination paper on Middle English. I was also lucky to have Tolkien's son Christopher as my tutor in that subject, and his teaching certainly helped me get a tolerable pass mark in the paper. JRR himself was the Chairman of the Examining Board the year of my graduation. I took my turn sitting in front of him and his academic colleagues for the "viva," which was the final moment of assessment for the student exhausted by a week writing papers on the whole of the three-year syllabus.

Some time after I came down, I was in Cambridge visiting a girlfriend who was touring in a theatre company playing in what Oxford snobbery called "the other place." It was a bright summer's day, and we were having tea in the gardens of the popular restaurant that overlooks the river, when I suddenly espied none other than Professor Tolkien himself who was standing, hands behind his back, watching the undergraduates punting on the Cam. I went up to him and politely made myself known. "And what do you think of Cambridge?" the great man asked. I mumbled some cliché about how beautiful it was. "Mind you," he replied, "behind this facade, they lead fearfully squalid lives. I am staying at King's and the breakfasts are truly dreadful." He clearly relished this bit of Oxbridge nonsense and, although he kept a straight face, I am sure that he took it no more seriously than I did.

When I came down from University, I was very broke indeed with no family support possible. I was living out of a suitcase in a friend's apartment, and I had to get a job. I applied to the B.B.C., was interviewed and turned down. Many Oxbridge arts graduates found their way into advertising agencies. So I sat down and wrote job application letters to a number of the leading agencies in the business.

In St. Martin's Lane was an old established ad agency called the London Press Exchange. I went for an interview there, having only the haziest idea of what advertising was really about. I was interviewed by a man named Cyrus Ducker, an important, high-profile director of the agency who subsequently became one of the leading figures in the creation of commercial television as an advertising medium. Cyrus was very kind and talked at great length, although most of what he said went over my head. I said precious little, but at the end of the interview he offered me job as an assistant to an account executive, whatever that was.

My immediate boss was one David Dutton whose father had invented a system of shorthand, popular at the time and said to be simpler than its competitor, Pitman's. David looked after many of the prestigious accounts handled by the LPE. A rather genteel, old-fashioned air permeated the agency. Saville Row suits, old Etonian ties and the odd hereditary title were commonplace. In the staff coffee room, senior executives would sit over their morning coffee with the *Times* crossword puzzle. Having but recently graduated, my mind was stocked with a plentiful supply of literary quotations that the *Times* puzzle at that time used in abundance, so I became a quite acceptable member of the club.

I went on holiday to Majorca where I stayed in Palma with Martin Seymour-Smith. Martin's wife Janet, who was also a fellow undergrad at Oxford, was working with Robert Graves on his monumental work on Greek Myths. I met Robert and Beryl Graves at Martin's flat. The grey-haired patriarchal figure of the great poet and novelist was rather awe inspiring, but both he and Beryl were warm and friendly and not in the least condescending or patronising, and I was invited to stay a week with them at their home in Deya, on the north coast of the island. Subsequently, I met Robert and Beryl a few times when they were in London, and one Easter at a fair on Hampstead Heath, Robert insisted that I had my fortune told by the gypsy woman whose tent we were walking by. As Robert insisted on paying for it, I could hardly refuse and, when I came out a few minutes later, he asked me what she had said. I told him she had predicted that one day I would have my own business, which I thought was highly unlikely. Robert decided to go in himself, and the family and I waited outside wondering what the result would be. Robert came out laughing heartily. She had said exactly the same to him.

I saw my first bullfight in Palma and became addicted to *el arte del toreo*. I read Hemingway's *Death in the Afternoon* and *The Sun Also Rises*, as well as any other book I could find on the subject. There were heated arguments with friends, who saw the corrida as a cruel sport and could not understand how I, an animal lover, could condone it. And yet, some of them found no problem whatsoever with the idea of twenty or thirty horsemen and women in red coats galloping around the English countryside with a pack of dogs in pursuit of a miserable frightened fox. I would try to explain that the corrida was about human courage facing possible death on the horns of a special breed of fighting animal that would die in combat, quite unlike the domestic cattle that were slaughtered in cold blood to supply those juicy steaks on the dinner table.

Whenever possible I went to major bullfight festivals in Seville, Madrid, Valencia, Malaga and other cities on the seasonal circuit. I saw Luis Miguel Dominguin, Antonio Ordonez and all the other great toreros of the time. A couple of times I ran with the bulls during the San Fermin fiesta in Pamplona, and it happened that, on one occasion, I was seen doing it by an acquaintance whom I had met once in London. He told a mutual friend so that news of my courage got back to London before me. When I pointed out that one could run through the streets of Pamplona and into the bull ring with reasonably complete safety provided one started well ahead of *los toros*, it was taken as false modesty. Any sensible foreign aficionado who just wanted to enjoy the fun did this, of course, and jumped over the *barrera* around the ring before the bulls actually arrived.

At the Malaga feria one year, I briefly met the great Orson Welles who was drinking in the bar of a fashionable hotel near the bull-ring, surrounded by admirers. Welles, I knew, was planning to make a film about bull-fighting. I then wrote to him offering to work for nothing on the picture in any capacity, but I never heard back and the film was never made, presumably because he couldn't raise the finance.

With *el arte del toreo* as my subject, I appeared on a popular television quiz show borrowed from America called *The $64,000 Question*. I certainly did not expect to last the whole way, but I hoped to go taking a reasonable large amount of loot with me. My subject was far from popular with the audience, judging from some fairly abusive mail I received. Perhaps this was why my questions got noticeably harder, and I was disqualified a bit earlier than I had originally anticipated. Ken Tynan, who certainly knew more about the subject than I did—he had written a book about it—then appeared on the programme answering questions on jazz, which I certainly knew more about than him. I got some malicious satisfaction out of the fact that he went down on his first session because he didn't know Coleman Hawkins' classic recording of *Body and Soul.*

As Spain and Andalusia particularly became a popular holiday area, the bullfight became more corrupt and tailored to the tourist trade. I am afraid than my passion for the corrida has now faded away totally.

I did, however, buy a flamenco guitar and got interested in the *cante jondo*, which grew out of its similarity in content to blues music. That is a love of Andalusian culture that has never faded at all.

After a short time at the LPE, I managed to move over to what was known as their Screen and Radio Department to produce cinema ads and radio programmes. That, I suppose, is where my journey to realise my dream of becoming a film director really began. The office I shared overlooked the Coliseum Theatre where at that time all the great American musicals were staged in London. My job was to record programmes and direct the actors hired to do the commercials. For a series of spots advertising carpets, the copywriter had created an avuncular salesman character; I found an actor named Arthur Lowe who played the part impeccably. He later worked at the Royal Court Theatre before achieving national fame playing Captain Mainwaring (pronounced "Mannering"), the pompous bank manager who commanded the Home Guard volunteers in the television sit-com, *Dad's Army.* I also managed to sell to Macdougalls—the leading British flour company—the idea of a programme featuring the guitar group led by Ivor Mairants, one of the leading jazz musicians in Britain.

The LPE was the first agency in Great Britain to handle the American Coca-Cola account. A high-powered team in Brooks Brothers suits came over from the U.S. advertising agency to indoctrinate us in a week of intensive briefing. What they gave us was, in fact, an intriguing piece of American social history. The first speaker opened by quoting President Eisenhower, who said that a baseball bat, a hamburger and a bottle of Coke symbolized the U.S.of A. We were then told the story of how Coke started in Atlanta, Georgia, where its inventor peddled it as some sort of nerve tonic, and we were shown examples of the many stages of Coke advertising. One brilliant illustrator did a series of Norman Rockwell-like still life paintings. When I asked why the series had come to an end, I was told casually that the artist had been investigated for un-American activities by the dreaded HUAC committee, which meant, of course, that the Coca-Cola Corporation could no longer employ him. We were given enormous books of guidelines and rules for the presentation of the classic Coke logo—the red disc with the words Coca-Cola—to dictate how it should appear in any advertising artwork and what angle would be right for the picture to prevent any danger of distortion. The London Coke chief was a nice man called Joe Baraldi, and I witnessed a moment in Coke history when Joe was on the phone to the States to get the go-ahead to acquire the Piccadilly Circus advertising site, which was the Number Two site in the Western World. The Number One site was, of course, Times Square in New York, and this, to the chagrin of the Coca-Cola Corporation had been grabbed by their arch rival, Pepsi-Cola. They had to have Piccadilly, and for many years after that, the big Coke neon sign looked down on the famous statue of Eros.

A Diversion Down the King's Road

We were now into the sixties—a time when the King's Road began to change its image from one of old-fashioned Bohemia to the swinging scene of miniskirts, bell-bottom trousers and flowered shirts; what George Melly called in the title of his book about it all, *The Revolt Into Style*. I confess that as a jazz and blues aficionado, of a slightly older vintage, I lived a sort of parallel existence to all this, paying it lip service, recognising the "scene" and, of course, exploiting its advertising potential, but not really being part of it.

During these years, I rented a bed-sitting room and a kitchen from Douglas Newton and Mary Lee Settle, two writers whom I had known when I lived in Well Walk, Hampstead, before I went up to University. They had taken a lease on a house in Sloane Court West, just off Sloane Square, and, without having a regular income, at that time they were both struggling. Letting out rooms in this large house gave them some sort of financial stability. The atmosphere in Sloane Court West was both relaxed and serious. My fellow lodgers included the anthropologist, Jim Spillius, who went off to be advisor to the Queen of Tonga, and various usually out of work actors and aspiring writers. Artists like Eduardo Paolozzi and Bill Turnbull, as yet unrecognised, were frequent visitors, as well as Christopher Logue and the maverick American film maker, James Broughton. Mary Lee had had a copy of the record album of a modern beggar's opera—*Guys and Dolls*—sent over from the States sometime before it opened in London, and we were all hooked on this wonderful musical realisation of Damon Runyon's New York. We knew all the lyrics off by heart. When the show arrived at the Coliseum, I got seats for the first night as soon as the box office opened. Sam Levene, whom I had seen in many gangster movies, played Nathan Detroit, organizer of the only "permanent floating crap game in New York," the role played by Frank Sinatra in the movie. Vivian Blaine was Adelaide, which she also played in the film, and Stubby Kaye was there, too, telling everybody to "sit down and stop rockin' the boat." The whole evening was unforgettable magic. Later Douglas and Mary Lee separated and both went to America. Douglas became the director of the New York Museum of Primitive Art, and Mary Lee, who was American, returned to her roots and became a distinguished novelist.

About this time I had my first encounter with the world of horror film production, in the person of beautiful American actress Ramsay Ames. Ramsay had started her career specializing in Latin-American dance and she also took up singing, but she suffered a back injury which ended her dancing work. Then, by chance, as she was passing through LA airport on a visit to her mother there, she was noticed by Harry Cohn, the president of Columbia Pictures. The meeting resulted in a screen test and her first film called *Two Senoritas from Chicago.* From Columbia she went to Universal where she starred in such offerings as *The Mummy's Ghost* with Lon Chaney Jr. and John Carradine. She made a lot of movies after that, including a couple with Gilbert Roland, but she never managed to break out of B features. When her contract with Universal expired, she seemed to have finished with Hollywood and she left the scene and came to England. I met her at a party given by my old jazz-loving friends. She had come to the party with the lovely jazz singer, Marie Bryant, with whom she was staying (Marie later recorded with Humphrey Lyttleton). Ramsay and I saw quite a lot of each other, having discovered our shared love of flamenco music and bullfighting. I arranged for her to have a guest appearance on my Ivor Mairants programme, and she sang a number for which she wrote lyrics in Portuguese. But she now seemed uncertain where she was going and there did not seem to be any kind of future for her in England, so she decided to go to Spain and I saw her off at Heathrow airport. A week or two later, a friend sent me a cutting from a Madrid newspaper with a picture of Ramsey in torero costume singing at the Castellana Hilton Hotel. She stayed for some years in Spain where she had her own television interview show, appeared in the odd film, including Sir Carol Reed's thriller, *The Running Man*, and married the playwright Dale Wasserman, who wrote *The Man from La Mancha*.

Terence Conran had rented a room in Douglas and Mary's Sloane Court West house before I arrived there. For a while he still used the basement for making some of his early coffee house furniture, for this was the beginning of the coffee bar era in London. The first coffee bar in the King's Road, and one of the first anywhere in London outside of Soho, was the Fantasy, owned by a chap named Archie McNair. He was a great friend of Mary Quant and Alexander Plunkett Greene and was involved with them in their King's Road fashion boutique, Bazaar. The rest, as they say, is history.

For the price of a cup or two of coffee, one could spend a pleasant evening in Archie's place, where people like Alexis Korner would drop by and play guitar and sing the blues. Flamenco was performed, too, which as I mentioned earlier had become a great passion of mine. The regulars at the Fantasy included actors like Denholm Elliott, with whom I was later to work on my first feature movie, and the immensely talented Donald Cammell, who wrote and directed *Performance*. Donald, who wore

Ramsay Ames

elegantly tailored "teddy boy" suits that contrasted dramatically with his public school accent, was a successful portrait painter in the classic tradition beloved by public dignitaries. His large studio off the King's Road was a regular party venue, always adorned by beautiful girls from the London art schools, and at Donald's studio I met my first wife Fay.

Joaquin Gomez, a flamenco guitarist who had a phenomenal technique, often turned up at the Fantasy with a singer, Rafael Rodriguez. I took lessons from Joaquin on Saturday mornings in my flat. I also took lessons with other visiting flamenco guitarists and spent much time with the flamenco community in London. When dance companies came to perform, there was always open house at the studio house in Belsize Park where Fay and I lived after we were married, which meant a lot of memorable *juergas*—parties.

I did manage some sort of expertise playing flamenco, and one evening I was rung up by one Ron Hitchens, a colourful Cockney chap who earned his living selling shirts in Petticoat Lane in London's East End. Ron, once described by a critic reporting on a television programme that featured him as a "sprightly Hogarthian character," was a man of many talents, not least among them his extraordinary energy on the dance floor. He had won a championship for dancing non-stop for twenty-four hours, maybe longer. He then took up flamenco dancing. His mother was Chinese, and he did have a passably gypsy appearance. In the West End he worked in many clubs and Spanish restaurants. One of his most lucrative gigs was at a club called the Casino de Paris in Soho, where he and his partner did an act in the late cabaret show. His regular guitarist was a highly regarded Spaniard named Antonio Navarro who had given me a number of lessons. Antonio, it transpired, had taken sick on the evening in question, and Ron wanted me to "dep" for him. I protested that I really was not good enough to do the job. Ron insisted that if he gave me the routines for the dances they performed I could manage it, and the situation was desperate. Now the thing about flamenco is that it is based on a number of set patterns and rhythms. I knew these forms and how to play them, but, of course, I would not be able to match Antonio's solo expertise, and so my playing would be pretty basic. With some apprehension, I turned up at the club that evening and made my way through a big dressing room full of nubile, six-foot showgirls, all in a state of semi-nudity, to the tiny dressing room which Ron shared with his partner Janet. Ron made all her flamenco costumes, another of his many talents. He gave me a quick breakdown on the dances they were performing—a *Sevillanas,* an *Alegrias* and a *Seguirya*—and I donned the Andalusian suit that Ron lent me which more or less fitted.

Somehow or other I managed to get through the evening adequately. To my surprise Antonio agreed that if I wanted to, I was welcome to sit in for him on the gig one night a week. Feeling rather flattered, I said okay and turned up every Monday night for the rest of their stint at the club. The clientele seemed on the whole to be "visiting firemen," salesmen of various kinds on a night out on the town. One evening a little confrontation occurred with a drunk customer that looked as though it might terminate Ron's contract rather earlier than planned. Ron and Janet were into their final number—a *seguiriya*, which is a slow and dramatic flamenco form. At this moment the well-oiled diner, who had been barracking since the beginning of the act—presumably he wanted more of the showgirls and not this Spanish stuff—began to get loudly abusive and even advanced towards the stage, having to be pulled back to his table by the waiters. I could see that Ron was getting angrier by the minute, but we ploughed on through the number to the end. At that point, Ron picked up his black *sombrero cordobes,* which he threw to the floor during the routine, hurled it at the drunk, and leapt off the stage, shouting "I'll break your fucking neck!" It must have astonished the audience who probably thought that Ron was a genuine Spanish gypsy, and he, in his turn, had to be restrained by the waiters. Janet ran off the stage in tears, followed by myself thinking that this was certainly the end of the gig, but the management were extremely understanding, and the act continued until the end of the contract.

There used to be a prestigious flamenco night club in

Madrid called La Zambra, and I spent wonderful evenings there whenever I was in that city. It never catered to the tourist trade and was uncompromising in its presentation of the music as a serious and profound art form. Its *cuadro* featured some of the most famous singers of the day, including Pericon de Cadiz and Manolo Vargas.

Duende is something very important to the art of flamenco. The word means "the spirit," and when the singer of the cante is possessed by the *duende*, then his or her work will reach the highest emotional and spiritual expression. It does not always happen and depends on the mood of the artist, the atmosphere, his surroundings, the communication between him and his audience and all sorts of subtle and important elements devoutly to be wished for at the moment he begins to sing. Without the *duende* then, however technically brilliant the cantaor, however profound his knowledge of the cante hondo or deep song, something will be missing. When the *duende* descends on the artist, then the deep and almost religious mysteries of this extraordinary folk music will be passed on to the audience.

One year the cuadro flamenco from *La Zambra* came to London to appear at the Hippodrome Theatre, and I reviewed the show for *The Melody Maker*. I and my friend Gerald Howson, who had written a brilliant book called *The Flamencos of Cadiz Bay*, got to know Pericon de Cadiz, Manolo Vargas and their guitarist Andres Heredia, and one evening they honoured us with an impromptu juerga at Mall Studios. I had passed on my enthusiasm for the music to my friend, Ivor Mairants, who was at this time running a most successful guitar school and music shop in Soho. I had earlier introduced Ivor to my first flamenco teacher, Joaquin Gomez, and as a result, Ivor produced the first book on flamenco guitar playing in English.

I suggested to Ivor that it would be great if we could record the *Zambra* stars while they were in London. Pericon, Manolo and Andres were willing, so Ivor and I organised and financed a recording session at a small studio in Bond Street. For five minutes, I was a record producer and the album, called *Flamenco Gitano* (Cadiz Flamenco), appeared on the Oriole label. I wrote the sleeve note, Gerald did the front cover photograph and Ivor and I supervised the recording session. It was really a labour of love, and we did not see a penny back on the venture. Sadly, I later got some playback that the flamencos thought that we had made money out of the album and were angry that they had received nothing from it apart from a small fee for the session.

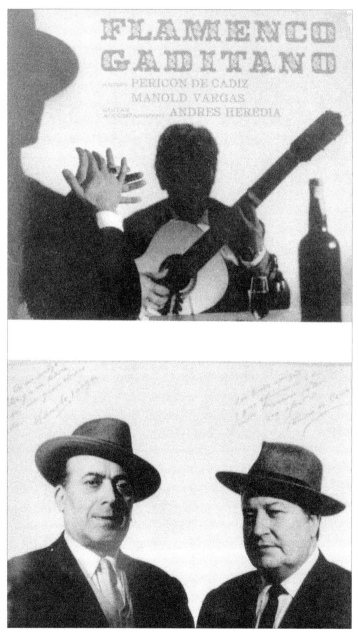

Manolo Vargas,Pericon de Cadiz and the LP cover.

The Actual Beef Cube

The LPE made a series of cinema advertisements for Coca-Cola written and produced by the advertising film company Pearl and Dean. Shot in colour, they had a "jingle" music track, written by Steve Race and sung by Alma Cogan, and they were to be filmed by a French director in the south of France. I went along as agency representative and even appeared in one of the spots as a waiter offering a Coke to Byron Lloyd, the creative head of Pearl and Dean. Byron offered me a job as a production assistant and I leapt at it.   Pearl and Dean, the top cinema advertising company in the business, handling both distribution and production, had offices in Dover Street. Their logo heralding the ads—a shot of a classic Greek temple inspired by the Parthenon—was to be seen at every performance in every cinema in Britain, apart from the Rank circuit, of course. The company was run by Ernie Pearl, a large expansive character, and Bob Dean, a tall, spare and elegant man of great charm. The basement viewing theatre, where the films they made were shown to the clients, was decorated like all the other Wardour

Street viewing theatres of the time. The walls were papered in dark red regency stripes, and the lighting was in a matching style. On one occasion, a client, a fairly high profile man named Dan Ingman, who had moved out of broadcasting into the advertising world and was heading up the visual media department of one of the large London agencies, was looking around at the decor as he waited patiently for the projection to start. He remarked that the theatre looked a bit like a tart's boudoir and then added that, as we were prostituting the art of film, this seemed quite appropriate.

Byron Lloyd was developing the production side of the company and was quite prepared to take the odd chance. He hired a collection of relatively untried writers, directors and producers. Among them were Douglas Rankin, an ex-wartime officer in the Indian army who had made one half-hour travelogue about Capri, Jim Garrett, an assistant director from British Transport Films who went on to head his own successful production company that I later worked for, Pat Kelly, a feature film assistant director, and Tony Shaffer, a Cambridge law graduate who became a close friend socially and professionally. Later, of course, Tony became famous for his play *Sleuth* and many distinguished screenplays, including some of the Agatha Christie thrillers and *The Wicker Man*.

Byron gave me my first chance to direct a film, even though it was only a cinema advertisement. It was a musical short for something called *Sun Pat Raisins*. Steve Race, whom I got to know well, again wrote the soundtrack, and it starred a lovely American singer named Mildred Smith who was appearing in a West End review at that time. Surprising as it may now seem, at that time it was extremely difficult to get into the film technicians union—the A.C.T as it was then known. It was a sort of Catch 22 situation: you couldn't get a ticket unless you worked in the industry, and you couldn't work if you didn't have a ticket. However, if you were working for an advertising film company, it was somehow possible to wangle a ticket, and I managed to get one.

In those days most of the technicians used in making commercial spots for cinema, or commercial television when it started, came from the feature film industry. Although the medium provided a handy source of income during hard times in the British film industry—which were frequent—some of them were fairly cynical about it at first. In the end professionalism prevailed, and commercials gave people like me the opportunity to work with some of the most famous cinematographers in the business—artists like Geoff Unsworth, and Bob Krasker, who photographed *The Third Man* and many other great first feature movies. Some film technicians, who had retired wounded from the feature world, settled for full-time employment in the commercials business. Later generations of TV commercial makers often disparage the "old sweats," but they did provide the foundations of what was to become a hugely profitable business. Over the next few years, I directed a great many commercials and learnt much about the various techniques of film making from these old industry sweats. The TV commercials business was now in full swing, and from Pearl and Dean I moved to another production company called Guild Television. The producer at GTS was Ray Elton, a wise and knowledge-able ex-cameraman, bravely outspoken, who enjoyed life tremendously and had probably ruined his chances of a long and successful career in the feature business because he was never afraid to say what he thought. Ray, above all others, taught me most about the grammar of film mak-ing. Tony Shaffer came along for the ride, too, and moved in and out of agency and film company employment, as well as another old friend from the King's Road coffee bar scene, Gareth Bogarde, Dirk's younger brother, who had moved over from working in film editing.

> *Ring-a-Ring of roses*
> *Coronary thrombosis*
> *Expense account, expense account*
> *We all fall down.*

In the advertising world it was the strawberry season all year-round. To work successfully with the agencies, it was necessary to have a great number of expensive lunches, always, of course, paid for by the film company touting for business. Fortunately for me, despite the expensive over-eating, I managed to survive it with my health intact. Red wine is believed to be beneficial to the system, and I like to think that all the expensive claret I consumed was good for my arteries, if not for my bank account, for I developed a lifelong devotion to the stuff along with a superficial knowledge of wine mystique that enabled me to bullshit my way through many a dinner party. Then during production meetings with the agency and the client, we sat around a large table and discussed in detail and with high seriousness a thirty second spot for cat food, lipstick or whatever, with all sorts of high-flown cultural references ranging from Miles Davis to Monet, which we hoped would impress the client with our professional dedication, nay love even, for his product and its presentation in visual form. One agency producer named Peter Marsh, an ex-actor married at one time to Pat Phoenix, a star of the early days of the indestructible TV soap *Coronation Street*, would give us a bravura performance at these meetings, acting out with great brio the full dramatic and selling potential of the agency script. Embarrassing though it might be for we film makers, it no doubt impressed the client. Later, Peter Marsh became the head of a successful agency, and television companies usually trundled him on when they wanted an expert from the industry to make pronouncements on its place in society.

All cinema advertisements were filmed in colour on

35mm film, but with the arrival of commercial television, in the days before colour TV became the standard, it was back to the use of black and white. Screens were much smaller as well, hence the received wisdom that television was a close shot medium. Over the years TV ads have changed in style according to the mood of the moment. In the beginning one was usually trying to tell a story in narrative form in one minute or thirty seconds. I learned how to tell a story economically, and how to compose a frame that was both pleasing and dramatically effective. Much of the work I had to do for soap powders, floor cleaners and the like was unbearably dull, but some campaigns were a pleasure to work on. I remember with some affection a series for the white chocolate called Nestle's Milky Bar. The advertising agency writer had dreamt up a character called the Milky Bar Kid, a little boy in National Health glasses and a cowboy suit living out a little boy's Western fantasies. To the punch line "The Milky Bars are on me!" he distributed the product to his happy friends, all dressed up as cowboys and cowgirls, too. We decided to make tiny *homages* to the great John Ford, set in western saloons, on the railroad and the prairie. In one spot, where the Milky Bar Kid held up a stage coach, I had all the kids playing the passengers dressed like characters from one of the greatest Westerns that Ford ever made.

I also shot a notable series for the washing powder Omo that was quite different from the usual dreary deter-

A Milky Bar commercial - pretending to be John Ford.

gent advertising. Each commercial was a little anecdote in which the main character happened to wear a gleaming white garment. The product appeared only at the end in what was called the pack shot. Casting these spots always took place with the agency present and probably the client too. When the poor actors turned up to be interviewed, they were disconcertingly faced with a row of people staring intently at them but mostly saying nothing. Much later, the casting director told me that an actor who had been unsuccessful in getting a role in one of these Omo commercials was Terry Stamp. On another occasion, a commercial we made with Tony Selby, later well-known as a Cockney character actor, was never shown because the client felt that Tony looked too Italian.

At that time high profile actors were loath to be involved in commercials without the use of an on-screen title that gave their name or a voice-over introduction to make perfectly clear that they appeared as themselves to endorse the product, not just as jobbing actors playing a role. And they weren't particularly keen on doing it anyway. In their view, it looked as though they were on the slippery slope or desperately hard-up, but sometimes a fat cheque could concentrate the mind wonderfully. Also a sign of the times was that when you took a film unit out on the streets, rubber-necking bystanders would more likely ask you what product you were advertising rather than what movie you were making. The TV commercial could also make audiences familiar with actors' faces, and they could be recognized in the street for their association with a candy bar or a soap rather than for their more distinguished, if perhaps less financially rewarding, work in the theatre, which was another reason why many actors would not appear in them. My friend, Ray Elton, directed a series for a brand of instant coffee called Chico, and the artist featured in the spots was the wonderful Yvonne Arnaud, so distinguished for her work on stage that there was an Yvonne Arnaud Theatre in Guildford. She lived in Brighton, and one evening after returning from a day in London, the ticket collector at Brighton railway station

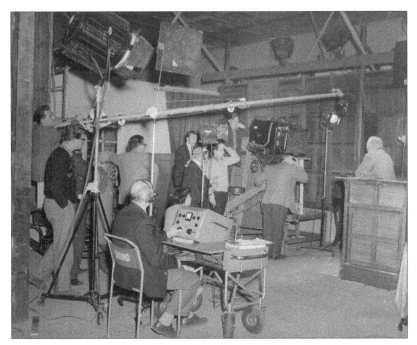

A comedy cinema ad for Jaffa Oranges. The actor behind the lamp stand is my friend John Schlesinger, the film director.

recognised her and said, "Oh you're the lady in the Chico coffee commercials, aren't you?."

Comedians were on the whole a lot less worried about this kind of publicity. I shot series with Peter Sellers, Roddy Maude-Roxby, Ken Connor and Sid James, the later two stalwarts of the *Carry On* series, and many others who were all a delight to work with.

A long series of spots for eggs featured the actor-manager Bernard Miles playing his rustic sage (which he did as a one-man music hall act), advising us all to "go to work on an egg." One Saturday morning, for some reason or other that may have been about Miles' availability, we were to shoot a simple one-shot fifteen-second script with Miles sitting at the breakfast table. He was late arriving at the small studio in Barnes where we were filming. In the meantime, I had set up the camera position and arranged the properties on the table in a way that looked fine for camera. The cinematographer lit the set and everything was ready to go. Bernard Miles finally turned up wearing his rustic garb, sat down at the table, rearranged all the props, gave us a nod, and we shot take one. That was it. Satisfied with his performance, Mr. Miles got up, said goodbye and left. As far as I was concerned, take one was okay by me, too, but I would have liked the courtesy of having been asked, and, as he must have known full well, the camera always needs to be checked before an artist leaves the set. I suppose he felt that advertising was a bit beneath him, but the money was quite acceptable, I am sure.

I have always regretted not having any real talent as a musician. I played jazz guitar but not too well, and I had a short affair with a tenor saxophone, although I soon realized that I was no threat to my idols, Coleman Hawkins and Lester Young. But I have listened to music constantly in my life, and I have always had a big involvement in the music on the soundtracks of my films. I sometimes was able to devise sequences with a certain piece of music or a musical style in mind, and I have always believed that the composer should be brought into the picture early on in the film making process, but this sadly this does not often happen. The result is that films are often cut with little concern for music and the poor composer finds he has been left without enough space to lay in the music properly. Sometimes this is a matter of no more than a few seconds, but if the film cannot be re-cut to allow this important space, then the damage has been done.

Early in my commercial making days, I was able to use a number of jazz musicians to compose tracks for me, and I got to know Ronnie Scott, Stan Tracy, Tubby Hayes and many other front rank players on the British jazz scene. One morning at a recording session for a documentary film I had shot, composer Steve Race made me a present of Gil Evans' great recording of Gershwin's *Porgy and Bess* featuring Miles Davis on flugelhorn, and I fell in love with his big band style. I still have this now rather worn LP on my shelves even though it has been replaced by a CD copy along with their other great collaboration, *Miles Ahead*. I had long wanted to use this style of jazz composition as a film backing track, and the opportunity came when I made a series of cinema advertisements for a brand of menthol cigarette called Consulate.

The Consulate cigarette copy line was "cool as a mountain stream," and each year they produced an expensive series of colour films illustrating this idea. This particular year the location was Lynton and Lynmouth in

Devon, and I had spent a month down in Devon with a film crew headed up by Billy Williams, who went on to a distinguished feature career, photographing many great movies. We sat around patiently waiting for the sun to back light the water. The end result looked pretty indeed with the handsome young models posing against verdant watery backdrops and jumping gaily over stiles, wandering romantically through wooded slopes, hopping hand-in-hand over stepping stones and, at the end, puffing happily on their cigarettes as they sat by the cool running streams of idyllic North Devon.

The jingle composer, Johnny Johnson, wrote a *Consulate* music theme that was obligatory to use on the films. The trouble was that it did not work for the light gay mood of the first part of the films. I thought Tubby Hayes, who had done a number of music tracks for me, was just the man to create the right sort of mood and sound, and I met Tubbs in a Soho pub where, over a couple of beers, we talked about the project and my wish for the Gil Evans sound. The only requirement was that for the last fifteen or so seconds of the ads, when the cigarettes came out and we went in for the close shot of the actual packet, he had to modulate into the recognised *Consulate* theme.

The line-up of musicians at the recording session was impressive indeed: it included not only Tubbs himself on tenor sax but also Ronnie Scott and just about every other jazz star on the London scene at that time, including the fine West Indian guitarist Ernie Ranglin whose solo on one of the films won great acclaim in his native Jamaica when the ad appeared in cinemas there.

The one person who was not happy with the result was, predictably, Johnny Johnson, who did not forgive me. When the films were shown to the clients, initially some consternation was felt among them, too, as they did not instantly hear their beloved jingle tune, although one of them professed to hear references to it in the lovely scores that Tubbs had written. So the all-important "suits" were satisfied in the end.

For the agency, Foote Cone and Belding, I made a couple of song and dance cinema ads that were great fun to shoot and quite spectacular. John Dankworth composed the music tracks, and Cleo Lane sang the words. At this time the musical *West Side Story* was running in a London theatre, and we used dancers from the show, as well as getting Chita Rivera's husband Tony Mordente, who played one of the Sharks, to choreograph the numbers.

As television advertising flourished and the production companies prospered, shooting on overseas locations became popular. This became attractive for a number of reasons, the first of which was, of course, the weather. When you wanted sun for a location shoot, you might well not get it in the U.K., and if you had to shoot in the winter to get a commercial on the screen for the spring, then your chances were even smaller. So it became practical to go overseas with the added plus that, if you needed a holiday situation to sell your product, foreign locations were exotic, beaches were long and the sea blue. Naturally, the South of France was popular. While I was down near St. Tropez, shooting a series with a French camera crew, and wandering around the shops on the port, I found one that belonged to a large, cheerful man who looked rather like a popular Jewish cockney actor named Alfred Marks. He not only looked like Alfie Marks, but also sounded like him, for, to my surprise, he spoke with a true East London accent. He was, he told us, the only soldier in the French Army during the war who couldn't speak a word of French. His family were on holiday in France when he was born, and his parents had not bothered to register him as English, with the result that he got called up by the Free French forces in England, which is how he ended up running this rather nice boutique in St. Trop. On his shelves, I noticed some rather attractive polo neck sweaters that were becoming fashionable wear for young women. "Ah," he said, "do you know how that happened? This dishy bird came into the shop, saw these great chunky blokes sweaters, took a fancy to them, and put one on which came down well below her waistline. Do you know who it was?" "Brigitte Bardot," I answered quick as a flash. "You're right," he said. "And that started the fashion. I had the director from Marks and Spencer down here on his yacht in no time at all, and I couldn't keep up with his orders."

After the South of France, places further afield proved an attraction. Jamaica became a regular venue for the production company I was working with, and then South Africa. Of course, the unmentionable fact was that it provided a nice little perk for the agency producers who had no objection to virtually a holiday abroad at their client's expense. I once went to Jamaica when we had a unit shooting there, to do no more than a couple of shots for an exterior paint commercial that had to show a brilliantly white painted bungalow. We stopped off overnight in New York, which enabled the agency producer to visit a relative and might have had something to do with his choice of location in the first place. What we did not foresee was that in Jamaica the houses don't have chimneys because the weather is so temperate all the year round, they don't need them. I managed to find a bungalow where it was possible to shoot angles that did not show its chimney-less character. Another time I went to Johannesburg to film a series of commercials for Ilford film for the agency Foote Cone and Belding, and one or two other products were added in to make the package economically viable. Nic Roeg came with me as cinematographer, which was his profession before he managed to make the move over into directing. We had a great time together, but found the situation there, as it was still the time of apartheid, uncomfortable and extremely depressing. The whites only—*nie blankes*—signs on buses, trains and public conveniences, and the way so many black people with whom one worked would seldom look you in the eye, proved disturbing and sad. One evening for a joke, I rang Nic in his hotel room and, doing my best to imitate a South African accent, introduced myself as Sergeant Johannsen of the local CID. "I understand, Mr Roeg," I said, "that you have been making critical remarks in public about South Africa, and I would like to come round and talk to you about it." To Nic's eternal credit, he was not fazed in the least, and after a moment or two, I gave up the impersonation and began to laugh. Later in the hotel bar, Nic suggested we play the same joke on Chris, our American agency producer. During the time we had been in South Africa, Chris had often come on like a latter-day Abe Lincoln about the appalling nature of the regime, but, knowing my man as well as I did after making quite a few commercials with him, my reaction was immediate. "God, no," I said. "He's quite likely to protest his innocence and say he "hated those motherfucking niggers as much as they did,"" or something else unconscionable to that effect, and then where would we be for the rest of the shoot! Nic saw my point, but from time to time, as we circled around a swimming pool or worked on a beach in the hot afternoon sun, he would look over to me while Chris' attention was elsewhere and, with raised eyebrow and a wicked grin, make a telephone dialing sign.

Commercials were always expensive to shoot. The cost

per second of screen time was actually wildly in excess of feature film making costs. As commercials became flashier and visually astonishing, they made even the generous budgets we were enjoying in those days seem ludicrously small by comparison. Even then it sometimes seemed like taking a sledgehammer to crack a nut. At that time, a famous Rank Film Company trade advertisement appeared in the trade journal *Screen International*, that was a photograph of a major feature film unit—rank upon rank of technicians rather like a crowded school photograph with the director, the producer, the cinematographer, the production designer, the supervising editor and other key heads of department in the front row. We had a copy of this advertisement stuck on the wall in our office with a small bubble added above the director's head. It read, "Now we go in for the pack shot of the actual beef cube."

Hit the marks and don't bump into the other actors

Guild Television was one of a group of companies called the Film Producers Guild that had studios at Merton Park in South London. Apart from the commercials, I had also managed to make a number of sponsored documentary films with another of the companies in the group, and it was probably that work that got me my first cinema films. The Film Producers Guild was associated with the distributor Anglo Amalgamated, and made a lot of B-feature pictures and programme-filling short films. The most famous was the series known as *Scotland Yarders*, allegedly true crime stories introduced by the crime writer and journalist Edgar Lustgarten. The man who gave me my chance was producer Jack Greenwood. This was my introduction to the tough disciplines of low-budget film making, and what an education it was. These half-hour stories were shot in four or five hectic days and, every so often, Lustgarten would come into the studio, sit down at a desk in a small standing set, and deliver his on-camera narrative links with the aid of a teleprompter.

My first story, called *The Grand Junction Case*, was photographed by a cameraman I had worked with before named Arthur Lavis, and before shooting began, Jack called us both into his office and delivered a *diktat*. "I don't want any of this arty low-key lighting, Arthur," he said. "I've paid for the artists and I want to see their faces." A lot of industry and not much art, but it was an experience for which I was eternally grateful. It taught me to plan carefully the night before what I was going to shoot the following day and to think on my feet. I said "allegedly true" crime stories, and I think that some of the earlier ones may really have been that, but necessity became the mother of invention by the time I got in on the act. For example, I shot one script called *The Silent Weapon* in which the murder victim was killed by a boomerang that miraculously had returned to the murderer after scoring a direct hit—a likely story! Although the first *Scotland Yarders* I made were shot in black and white, the last two were shot in Eastman colour. One of them, *Company of Fools*, had such a daft story that I decided that the only way to do it was to play it for comedy. I cast Barrie Ingham and Maurice Kaufman in the leading roles, and some years later I was delighted to note it was still running as the support to a Goldie Hawn movie.

After shooting several of the *Scotland Yarders*, Jack

gave me a real B-feature movie to direct. It was one of the studio's other staple earners—their series of Edgar Wallace thrillers. It was called *Partners in Crime*, and I had the marvellous Bernard Lee as my star. The pressure to shoot fast was just as great; one had to shoot more footage on a slightly longer schedule. Jack's associate producer was a chap called Jim O'Connolly. One abiding memory, an echo in my mind, is one or the other of them standing on the edge of the set and asking, "Can we go?" in a plaintive and slightly threatening manner. When both of them were on the set together, they seemed to look at their wrist watches in synchronisation. Bernie Lee joked that they were actually in a race to see who could get his arm up quicker. The climax of the story involved an exploding lorry. As things were done on the cheap, the special effects department hadn't done too good a job on setting the charges, so when I shot the scene, the lorry did not explode in the spectacular fashion it was supposed to. It did, however, start burning. We cut the camera and waited - an agonising moment for Jim O'Connolly. Did he risk sending in somebody to put the fire out and save the lorry for another take or what? I confess to a malicious satisfaction that for once the decision was not mine to make, and the cameras crew and I surreptitiously grinned at each other.

So now I had made it at last. I was a real film director, and to my delight on a trip to Paris I found *Partners in Crime* showing at a Left Bank Cinema with the magic words on the poster, "Un film de Peter Duffell." Never mind that it was only a mediocre B-feature story and that it had been cut by a hack editor in the most primitive fashion possible. I was there and it was my work—well, more or less. But this was also, I am afraid, the time when my first marriage ended after five years. When the painful divorce was over, I married the actress Patricia MaCarron.

This was also the time of the end of the B-feature film. Many movie technicians were now making a living shooting drama series for television at major studios like Pinewood and Shepperton. One early and popular show was *The Avengers*. It had started as a live television show before being made as a black and white television series. The original leading lady, Honor Blackman, had left and was replaced by Diana Rigg, a beautiful and talented young actress from the Royal Shakespeare Company. The show was a great success in the United States where the Mrs. Peel character, in her kinky boots and fetishist leather gear, went down extremely well. The next series was shot in colour and went into production somewhat under-prepared due to a sudden demand from the States for more episodes. The result was a kind of organized chaos on the studio floor; several episodes were shot at once, the writers working under great stress to hand over new scenes to equally harassed directors minutes before filming. *The Avengers* had a rather camp visual style of its own, which I called "shooting through brandy glasses." Just before I arrived on the scene, Jack Greenwood, the producer at Merton Park Studios, was brought in to get some kind of order into the situation, and once again he gave me a chance to enter a new field that was, in fact, going to keep me gainfully employed for a number of years.

I took over from another director an episode called "The Winged Avenger," starring the wonderful and eccentric Irish actor, Jack MacGowran. On my first morning, Diana Rigg arrived on the set and her opening remark was "What do you want, Mr. Director?" This did not bode well for the future, but, as she was the star of the show and I was just a new boy, I swallowed my pride and politely explained to her what it was I needed her to do. Why she should be so aggressive I had no idea, but I had a feeling that it was because I was brought in by Jack who was viewed with suspicion by the stars of the show. Maybe it was just her own insecurity at that time and place. I also had a feeling that she did not really like the show that much, although she was certainly paid more money for it than she would be getting in the legit theatre, and it must have provided a nice financial cushion for her more serious career at the RSC. Her ignorance of film technique at that early stage in her career also became painfully clear one day when I was shooting a close-up of her in a scene with Patrick Macnee. Not understanding that, with the correct lens, the camera did not have to be right up her nostrils, she turned to me and said acidly something like, "Don't you ever shoot close-ups?" Patrick, always the peace maker, quietly pointed out that I certainly did. He, of course, always came to the daily rushes viewing, which she never did, so he knew exactly what I was up to.

I shot numerous additional scenes for other episodes, mostly with Diana and Patrick—and the brandy glasses, of course—the scripts for which were usually shoved in one's hand the morning of shooting. Then the executive producer, Julian Wintle, recommended me to Sidney Cole, who was producing for the Lew Grade organisation another series called *Man in a Suitcase*. Sidney was a man of great experience in the film industry as editor and producer, and had been an important member of the Ealing Studios team in its heyday. He worked on such classic movies as *The Man in the White Suit* and *Scott of the Antarctic*, after which he moved over to television series projects where he produced, among others, the *Robin Hood* series with Richard Greene and then *Danger Man* starring Patrick McGoohan. This latter series was intended to go into colour, and I had written a script for it called *Night in a Garden in Spain*. It was, alas, never made as Patrick decided to do no more episodes *of Danger Man* but instead made a remarkable series which became a cult classic, *The Prisoner*. So I went to meet Sidney at Pinewood Studios. He was an affable, unpretentious man, and he and I got on well. My agent soon received a contract for me to direct an episode of Sidney's current project.

Man in a Suitcase was a thriller series about a somewhat disenchanted ex-CIA man named McGill who had come to Britain to work as a private investigator. My episode was called "Burden of Proof," featuring Rupert Davies, a notable Inspector Maigret in an excellent television series. Fortunately Sidney was happy with my first effort, and I went on to direct episodes until the end of the series.

The daily schedule was usually based on pages and numbers of scenes. This produced what we called the "Indians attack the Fort" syndrome: the stage direction was one line of text, while the shooting of it could be incredibly complicated calling for a great number of camera set-ups. Good and bad moments occurred on *Man in a Suitcase*. As always, the best moments were when one managed to crack particularly difficult problems that may have been caused by inadequate scripting—underwritten characters or holes in the plot, for example—or quite simply an overloaded, back-breaking schedule that somehow you just had to get through on time. At the end of every day's shooting, the director would have a drink in the office with Sidney and his associate producer Barry Delmaine. One colleague of mine called this "the drink and dressing down session," because if you hadn't made the day's schedule the associate producer always had some caustic remarks to make and some unhelpful suggestions to solve the problem.

The most important relationship that a director has on

a movie is that between himself and his actors. I am talking about narrative drama cinema, not the current special effects and digitally manipulated Hollywood extravaganzas. It is the most important relationship because the actors are what the director has on the screen. They are his "faery gold." Without good performances from them, his film will fail artistically if not commercially. They are also his most difficult challenge because each one of them has his or her own personality and approach to the problems of performance, and the director's problem is to keep each one of his cast happy and confident that his or her talents are being shown fully on the screen. No director can turn a bad actor into a good one, or even a good actor into a great one, but by clever shooting and with the aid of a good editor (or cutter as the Americans used to call him) he can certainly turn a mediocre performance into a passable one. That is to say that since D.W. Griffith invented the close-up, film can particularise, emphasise and select at the will of the director. In the way in which the various pieces of film are put together, the director and his editor can even alter the effect and meaning of what has been recorded. The Russian film makers Pudovkin and Kuleshov made a famous demonstration of this principle which is recorded in Pudovkin's book on film technique and discussed at length in Karel Reisz's excellent *The Technique of Film Editing*. They took a close-up of a famous Russian actor and used it three times over. They joined the shot of the actor whose expression was neutral to shots of a plate of soup, a coffin in which lay a dead woman, and a little girl playing with a toy...

> *"When we showed the three combinations to an audience which had not been let into the secret the result was terrific,"* they wrote. *"The public raved about the acting of the artist. They pointed out the heavy pensiveness of his mood over the forgotten soup, were touched and moved by the deep sorrow with which he looked on the dead woman, and admired the light happy smile with which he surveyed the girl at play. But we knew that in all three cases, the face was exactly the same."*

They were, of course, working in the days of silent cinema, but to some extent what they worked out is still applicable. In fact, an actor's whole performance can be modified in the cutting rooms—speeded up, slowed down or even improved, although with actors of talent such manipulation becomes unnecessary and undesirable. That, after all, is not why they were cast in the first place. Another way in which the relationship can be difficult is if the director's interpretation of the script and the character differs radically from that of the actor. Omar Sharif told me that David Lean, who wielded immense power over his films, was said to ask a difficult star who was disagreeing with him whether he wanted to work on his film or not. These days, however, in Hollywood, the stars usually pick the director and not the other way round, in which case the director goes, not the actor. The final result, I suppose, is embodied by the famous remark that "the lunatics are taking over the asylum," originally made when Douglas Fairbanks and Mary Pickford started United Artists.

I've always been known as an actors' director and I enjoy working with them. Having done some acting myself, I can feel what it's like to be there in front of the camera. The director, Edward Dmytryk, in his excellent book *On Screen Directing*, had some wise insights on working with actors:

> *"Getting the best performance is often*
> *a highly emotional experience, both for*
> *the actor and the director. The two do not*
> *always see eye to eye, either in the area of*
> *characterisation or that of technique. One*
> *actor's working habits may be antipathetic*
> *to those of his fellow artists. Conflict may*
> *sometimes give rise to great art, but in*
> *a process as complex as film making,*
> *harmony can be a blessing."*

Dmytryk here quotes the difference between Glenn Ford and Marlon Brando: one actor at his best and most spontaneous in the first few takes, the other not knowing what he wants to do until he has tried a variety of approaches. Brando's acting technique was the technique of Richard Bradford, our American star of *Man in a Suitcase*. He had been spotted by Lew Grade in a Sam Spiegel movie called *The Chase*, in which he played a corrupt bank manager who, at a high point of the story, beat up the sheriff played by Marlon Brando. Richard himself was also a product of the Lee Strasberg Method School of acting, and he idolised Marlon Brando.

Much as I admired Richard for his dedication to finding the dramatic truth of what he was doing—sometimes rather difficult—and his concern with motivation, I have to say that it sometimes made work tough for a young director shooting under the extreme pressures of time and money, which are inevitable in low-budget television series. I did try, often with a written memo about character and motivation, to keep him as happy as possible, and I think he appreciated that. In his autobiography, *Songs My Mother Taught Me*, Marlon Brando expressed his own feelings about the problem:

> *"You can't fake it,"* he said, *"to find something in yourself that makes you feel pain, and you have to keep yourself in that mood throughout the day, saving the best for the close-up and not blowing it on the long shot, the medium shot, or the over-the*

*shoulder shot. You have to whip yourself into
this state, remain in it, repeat it take after
take, then be told an hour later to crank it
up once more because the director forgot
something. It takes an enormous toll."*

A film is seldom shot "in sequence" —that is to say,
starting at the beginning of the story and going on until
the end. We'd all like to do it that way, but it is, alas, only
devoutly to be wished for. A film is broken down into sequences, and each sequence is broken down into shots.
Financial considerations then demand that all scenes on
a specific location have to be shot one after the other
regardless of their place in the script. As Brando pointed
out, this does mean special problems for the actor in terms
of his emotional portrayal of a character. In the same day
an artist may have to show a character in various stages
of development, with bits missing in the middle and even
the wrong way round, and this is a problem that he or she
does not have to face on stage. The director can help, but
in the end the solving of the problem remains one for the
artist alone. The question now arises of how much of the
role the actor should learn. I once had an actress, new to
film, who turned up on the first day of shooting having
learnt the whole part off by heart. This was not too wise,
as I was in any case rewriting the script every night. Playing opposite her was a skilled film actor who hardly learnt

anything at all before he got on the set, but by the time we were ready to shoot, he was word perfect, and we usually got it in the first take. To quote Marlon Brando again:

> "When I first made movies, I memorised my lines from the script like other actors, or if the script was weak I'd improvise dialogue but still memorise it. I learned on my first picture The Men how easy it was to spoil your effectiveness in a picture by over-rehearsing and digging so deep into a part before filming began that you had nothing left to give when it counted.

> "This had taught me how fragile a characterisation can be on film and the importance of spontaneity, so after a while instead of memorising my lines by rote, I started trying to concentrate only on the meaning or thrust of a line during a scene, working from merely a suggestion of what it was about, and then improvising speeches as I went along so that they seemed spontaneous; the words might vary a little from those in the script, but audiences didn't know it."

Following the Brando philosophy, Richard's tendency

to do things that had not been planned in rehearsal and to change his dialogue at the last minute so that the other actors were uncertain of their cues often gave us terrible problems. Sometimes during a take, Richard would do something completely different from what we had rehearsed, which was particularly difficult for the camera operator who could never be quite sure where Richard was going to move. He also had a distressing habit of lighting up a cigarette during a shot, which he had not done in rehearsal and which could totally alter the ensuing action. He would even stand them on end on a desk in front of another character he might be interviewing, so that one's eyes were inevitably drawn towards the precariously balanced cigarette that might fall over at any moment. I once said to him jokingly that I was going to have a line written in for McGill to say when offered a cigarette by another character: "No thanks. I have given up smoking."

McGill was a loner and so the rest of the cast changed from episode to episode. The series has become something of a cult classic, recently re-released on television and now going out on DVD. I was interested that an episode called "Property of a Gentleman" rated high in a recent survey of the top five shows. I have one amusing memory of it. The story was built around an incredible art collection owned by an irascible old man played by Gordon Gostelow. His two crooked sons, played by Terence Alexander and Charles Hodgson, who were secretly selling off the paintings and replacing them with reproductions, try to bribe McGill by offering him one of the extremely valuable paintings. In the original script, McGill chooses a Monet and Terry Alexander had a line complimenting him on picking "my favourite Monet." Richard, however, decided that he did not like the painting we had chosen. So we all had to wait while he walked around the set and found a picture that he was happy with. As the walls of the set were covered with an astonishing number of the most famous paintings in the world—in reproduction of course—this took some time. He finally settled on a picture he liked, which turned out to be a Modigliani, so poor old Terry was faced with a bit of a tongue-twister. Charlie Hodgson was an old university friend of mine who had, among other roles, played Ariel in that famous Nevill Coghill production of *The Tempest* in Worcester College Gardens.

My own favourite episode, the last of the series, was called *The Revolutionaries*, and I wrote most of the script. In the story a character called Maza, a sort of Trotsky-like figure in exile in Sweden, played by a wonderful actor, Hugh Burden, had a passion for Beethoven piano sonatas and tells McGill how Lenin, while listening to *The Apassionata*, had famously said that Beethoven made one want to stroke people's heads, not hit them. To my delight, it turned out that Hugh could actually play the piano so we would not have to fake it; the only problem was that he couldn't manage the *Apassionata* at such short notice, but he could play the *Waldstein*. I said fine, *The Waldstein* it would be. I think Richard rather liked the episode, too, because of a shoot-out action sequence where he sprayed around a submachine gun to some effect! At one point during the filming when I really was up against it and had to finish on-time and schedule with no possibility of running over, Richard was being difficult about a piece of action that I had worked out with the stunt director, and my patience ran out. "For God's sake Richard," I said. "Trust me!" Richard approached me angrily. "Okay," I said, "hit me." But, of course, he didn't. He was actually quite a pussycat. He was always a most watchable presence on the screen, and one forgave him for sometimes being a bit of a pain in the butt. The magazine *ACTION TV* interviewed Richard in 2001 and it was only then that I discovered that he, when asked which directors he felt happy working with, had chosen Charlie Crichton, Freddie Francis and myself. Both Charlie and Freddie became much valued friends whose work I greatly admired. We had a splendid crew on *Man in a Suitcase*, and I hope they remember me with as much affection as I remember them.

I have seen Richard in many movies since those times, and in middle age he seems to have made a corner for himself in corrupt CIA men and New York police chiefs. I get the impression that he has sloughed off some of the method excesses of his earlier days.

After *Man in a Suitcase* I worked on numerous other

television series, interspersed with the odd foray back into commercials. I was shooting another series for Consulate Cigarettes in the Alpes Maritime in the South of France and working out of Victorine Studios in Nice. My friend Bryan Forbes was filming *The Mad Woman of Chaillot* there with Katharine Hepburn, Danny Kaye, Nanette Newman, Richard Chamberlain and a host of other big stars. I went to say hello to Bryan, who said he had recommended me to shoot an American comedy show called *The Ugliest Girl in Town* for Screen Gems Columbia. The ex-actor Jackie Cooper was executive producer and had asked Bryan if he knew any English directors who could shoot American-style comedy. Bryan had mentioned my name, which was kind of him as, although I had shot many comedy commercials, I had had no previous experience in the field at all. But what made my day was meeting the glorious Katharine Hepburn, who was on the set passing a large box of chocolates around to members of the crew. To my astonishment, when I turned up again five days later, after having finished filming to return our equipment to the studio, she remembered my name even though we had passed only a few words. One evening, at the Cap d'Antibes Hotel, I had dinner with Bryan and his wife, Nanette, and some of the other actors, including Danny Kaye, who insisted on making pancakes for everybody, which were quite delicious.

Back home, I went to meet the producer of the Screen

Gems series, one Jerry Davis. I took some odd reels of my work with me, but the fact that Bryan had recommended me was, it seemed, enough, and I did not have to prove anything. The basic concept of the show was that a hard-up fashion photographer, who could not afford to hire expensive models for his work, dressed up his kid brother Tim in drag and took stills of him. Unbelievably they are a great success, and so the deception has to be continued when they come to Swinging London. The running gag was how Tim, as the famous fashion model Timmy, could get out of drag to be with his girlfriend and not be found out. As the young actor playing the role did look like the ugliest girl in town, suspension of disbelief was certainly necessary if the audience were to accept his staggering success as a model. The show was the usual half hour sitcom format and shooting was the usual frantic battle against impossible scheduling. At that time it was normal for sitcoms in America to be shot in a television studio style, which is to say three fairly static video cameras running, one holding a master shot with all the action contained within the frame and two cameras picking up close shots. In the editing process canned laughter would be added to the sound track. This was the style understood by the producers of the show, but I had been trained in another discipline, to design my shots and pre-plan an editing sequence and, in the case of comedy, to make the comedy work by the proper use of editing.

A director from New York was brought over from the

States to show us Limey directors working on the show how to do it. He was an amiable chap who gloried in the name of Swackhamer. He did a lot of shouting on the set and covered a great deal of screen time efficiently and, I thought, quite boringly by using the television shooting style I have described. What he had to teach us I have no idea. One day I shot a fairly long tracking shot that the operator told me went wrong just before the camera stopped turning. I said it was okay as I intended to cut before that, and to my astonishment Jerry Davis, who was on the set watching the shooting, was enormously impressed.

On another occasion I had to shoot a complicated sequence of shots when our hero, for some outrageous plot reason, was in a woman's Turkish bath and was desperate to get out of it before it was his turn to be massaged by a terrifyingly butch lady masseuse. When we sat through rushes the next day, the front office were worried because they were not funny. I said, "Give my editing sequence to the editor back in L.A. and, if it isn't funny when the shots are cut together, then fire me." I went on working to the end of the show. *The Ugliest Girl in Town* was a belated attempt to cash in on the Swinging London Carnaby Street revolution, but it really came too late and was doomed from the start. It was never transmitted nationally in England, although I think it had a brief exposure somewhere in the Midlands, and it did not survive beyond its first series in the States.

I worked on another American TV comedy show called *A Bird's Eye View:* the adventures of a couple of zany airline hostesses, it starred the singer and comedienne Millicent Martin, one of the stars of the satirical television show *That was the Week that Was.* It was produced by a great character Sheldon Leonard, an actor turned producer who had hit the jackpot with shows like *The Beverly Hillbillies* and *I Spy.* I particularly remembered Sheldon for his great performance as Damon Runyon's Harry the Horse in the movie of *Guys and Dolls,* and it was a pleasure to meet and work with him. During his time in England, he drove around in a large white Rolls Royce of which he was clearly rather proud, and after lunch one day as we passed this splendid machine in its parking spot outside our studio block, I teasingly commented on what I thought was a nasty dent in the side door. Sheldon looked with horror at the vehicle. "Trick of the light," he said, "trick of the light," sounding delightfully like one of the Runyonesque heavies he had so often played on the screen. One of the episodes took place in Madrid where there was a sequence in a night club. I was able to cast my flamenco friends as the club musicians including the redoubtable Ron Hitchens whom I wrote about in an earlier chapter.

By now, my days in commercials were clearly numbered. I was too often away from the scene working on television series and trying desperately to get a real feature assignment, and people from the world of *Sixties'*

Chic were taking over. Fashion photographers like David Bailey and Terry Donovan were now used to direct commercials, and the hard fact was made clear to me one day by a rather obnoxious advertising agency producer, for whom I had worked on numerous occasions. I had shown him a reel of my latest work before taking him to a rather expensive Italian *trattoria*. During the course of lunch, he observed that I was using all the latest techniques, long focus lenses and so on, but that he couldn't use me any more because I wasn't fashionable. I felt like emptying his plate of expensive pasta over his head, but as I wished to remain on friendly terms with the restaurant management, I thought better of it.

Then came a Hitchcock-inspired series shot at the old MGM studios at Elstree. Called *Journey to the Unknown*, it was produced by Joan Harrison, married to the famous thriller writer Eric Ambler, who had worked on numerous projects with the great Hitchcock himself. But by the time I came on board, she had handed over the running of the show to Norman Lloyd, an ex-actor turned producer who had appeared notably as a villain in Hitchcock's *Saboteur*, clinging to the Statue of Liberty before falling to his death.

I was contracted to shoot a story about a teenage boy with strange supernatural powers that enabled him to command people to do things they had no power to disobey, causing a great deal of havoc and even death. He was under constant surveillance by some shadowy government department, and his parents, who knew of his powers, tried to limit his freedom of movement and were in a constant state of high anxiety. By chance, the boy meets a rather unsuccessful pair of showbiz people, a man and a woman, who, realizing his potential as a music hall and cabaret act, cold-bloodedly use the woman's attraction for the boy and set about exploiting his talents with terrible results.

When it came to casting, a certain rule had to be followed involving a points rating. In casting the major parts a score of one was required and there was a long list of approved artists, each one being given a whole or half a point. The ideal was to have one starring actor with a whole point, but an exception might be made when two actors with half a point each. (Dirk Bogarde, I noted, scored only half a point, not that there was a role that suited him in my movie). In the end our one-point actor was Janice Rule who flew over from the States to do the show. She had appeared in *The Chase* with Robert Redford and Richard Bradford, *The Swimmer* with Burt Lancaster and a host of other Hollywood movies. I found her warm and friendly and a consummate professional at all times on what was the usual hectic television episode shoot. For the strangely gifted boy, I found a new actor named Anthony Higgins—or Anthony Corlan as he then called himself—a young man with a special presence on the screen who later had a great success in Peter Greenaway's stylish and enigmatic film, *The Draughtsman's Contract*. As Janice's shifty partner, I cast Maurice Kaufman who had been in the *Scotland Yarder* which, because of its absurd plot line, I had played for comedy.

Around the same time, I was hired to do a much classier television series called *The Strange Report*, starring Anthony Quayle as Adam Strange, a private investigator with some odd idiosyncrasies and talents. His American sidekick, played by Kaz Garas, had a girlfriend played by Anneke Wills, at that time married to Michael Gough, whose son I had looked after as a vacation job in my university days. Tony Quayle was an actor for whom I have an undying affection and admiration. He had been the director of the Royal Shakespeare company at Stratford when he returned to civilian life after his wartime service. I first saw him at Stratford in a production of Shakespeare's chronicle play about King Henry the Eighth in which he played Bluff King Hal. His first entrance was funny. An empty throne sat centre stage with a host of courtiers and lords temporal and pastoral, all standing around looking rather uncomfortable. Then suddenly the King appeared rather surreptitiously from behind the throne, plonked himself down on it, and the play began.

During the War, Tony had a distinguished career in the Army and had been Intelligence Officer on the Rock of Gibraltar. He was there when the Polish General Sikorsky was killed in an air crash in the waters off the rock—later the subject of a notorious play by Rolf Hockhuth, who asserted Winston Churchill had ordered his assassination. Later in the war, he was dropped as a liaison officer with the Resistance in Albania, and he told me how he and his group had looked down on a village occupied by the retreating Germans and how that night he had slept in the same bed the German officer had used the night before. Tony was always a joy to direct, a man of great warmth and charm whose breadth of experience and knowledge was always gently and quietly passed on to those he worked with. In one episode the dramatic climax of the story was a confrontation between Adam Strange and a murderess who practised black magic in a ruined tower. The witch was played by Renee Asherson, who had played the French Princess wooed by Henry V in the classic Laurence Olivier film of Shakespeare's play. The script called upon her to show great fear in the scene, and Tony described to her the physical feelings of fear that he had experienced during the war. I realised that I, as director, was learning something, too, and I could not have helped her in the way he did on this occasion.

During the sixties and seventies, the London offices of the Twentieth Century Fox Film Corporation was helmed, as they say in *Variety* film jargon, by one Robert Goldstein, a film industry operator of the old school. Bob Goldstein knew absolutely everybody in the film business. He was an affable and relaxed character: easy to get on with, but underneath a charming exterior he was as tough and ruthless as he had to be to survive at the top. He had, I later found out, given Jack Cardiff a really hard time on the film of D.H. Lawrence's *Sons and Lovers*, starring Trevor Howard, which Jack directed. During Goldstein's years in London the company made the catastrophic decision to shoot at Pinewood Studios their new epic, *Anthony and Cleopatra*, starring Richard Burton and Elizabeth Taylor. Enormous sets were built, including the harbour at Alexandra, and one day, thanks to the production manager, Teddy Joseph, whom I knew quite well, I was taken on a tour of them and was duly impressed. But English weather had not really been taken into account, and the sun-bleached glories of the Nile could not be realised under the often grey skies of the Home Counties. Finally, admitting defeat, the production was moved to Cine-Citta in Rome, and the Pinewood sets broken down. Heads may have rolled as a result of this enormously expensive disaster, but Bob's was certainly not one of them, and he continued in office for some years after that. Somehow or other, largely due to friends of my wife, she and I were on the guest list for Bob's regular Saturday night private screenings in Twentieth's viewing theatre in Soho Square, where he ran the company's latest offerings. On Sundays, he held court at his large flat in Mayfair where he lived with his two sisters, known to the circle as "the girls," even though they were perhaps rather past the age at which that term could be honestly applied. But they were welcoming and enjoyed giving these brunch parties at which the main fare was always lox, bagels and scrambled eggs. A regular turnout came of Bob's London friends, businessmen and their wives not necessarily connected with the movie business, and also American film people who were visiting or passing through London. I remember one particular Sunday, as we sat around the table eating, somebody casually threw out that they had heard that Sean Connery had grown a moustache. "What sort of moustache?" asked one of the other guests. As I had seen the movie in which Connery had sported facial hair, I threw in my two pennyworths. "Like the one that Gregory Peck wore in *The Gunfighter*," I said. "Ah," retorted one of the other film moguls present, "that moustache cost Twentieth Century Fox several million dollars." I had always rated *The Gunfighter* highly in the Western canon, so I found this reaction somewhat puzzling at first, until he told me that the movie was a financial flop because audiences who adored Gregory Peck did not want to see him in any way different from the image of him that they fondly cherished, despite the film's positive reviews. I learnt another hard lesson about the film business that day. Times have changed, of course, and now an attractive female star can win an Oscar having, in the name of Art, disguised her beauty with a false nose and a generally "bad hair day" appearance. Mass audiences, however, probably still prefer to see Nicole Kidman as she appears in *Moulin Rouge* than in *The Hours*, so perhaps what the cynical producer said at Bob Goldstein's brunch party still holds true.

I met quite a few legendary characters at these Sunday morning sessions, but they were usually too concerned with their own projects to be interested in a young Brit film maker anxious to make a break into first features, and I have never had the enviable talent of self-promotion, so my sneaky hope that mixing with this circle might advance my career in some exciting way was not realised. Although I showed Bob Goldstein some of my work from time to time—even after I did break into features—I never managed to get a movie from him. So at that time, despite the B-feature movies at Merton Park, I had not really made it. I had written quite a few scripts, too, but none of them had found a market. During the 1960s and 1970s, the British film industry was in its usual need of intensive care, but one kind of movie that continued to be financially successful was the horror genre, and this was one of the possible ways into feature films. It turned out to be *my way*.

The Horror! The Horror!

From ghoulies and ghosties and long-legged beasties
and things that go bump in the night,
Good Lord, deliver us.

As the great Alfred Hitchcock said, "Fear is common to everyone. We are all born with fear from the chicken up. People like to be scared, they go on a roller coaster and scream and then get off giggling."

We enjoy being terrified from the safety of our cinema seats, secure in the knowledge that even the most terrifying monsters that erupted from the screen are made real only by our suspension of disbelief.

The classic horror movie did, I think, presuppose a belief—or at least a suspension of disbelief—in the Christian basis of society. The forces of good and evil in the movies tended to be the forces of God against those of Satan. There are, of course, rules of the game. Thus, if the crucifix is effective—as it was in all the classic vampire films— we suspend disbelief even though we may not be believers in the Christian faith or, come to that, in the existence of vampires and zombies or other forms of the "undead." We go along with the rules.

This set of mythical elements, which survived at least until the era of the films with Christopher Lee and Peter Cushing, no longer holds. Today's vampire movie will have a different set of conventions. Coppola's Dracula offered little or no reference to a Christian framework for the story. Other conventions are sometimes ignored, as for example the fact that Dracula cannot operate during the hours of daylight and has to return to his coffin before dawn. This basic part of the myth was, in fact, honoured in the breach some time ago, and perhaps in some Hammer films eventually, because the mechanics of the invented plots demanded it. But times have changed. Now Arnold Schwarzenegger or Batman is more likely to deliver us from the forces of evil than the good Lord, and, in the specific case of vampires, sometimes the crucifix, the garlic and the stake through the heart may still be required, but the karate expertise of Buffy the Vampire Slayer will be just as important.

At this time two British film companies, Hammer and Amicus, specialised in the horror genre. Hammer produced the *Dracula* movies, notable for the glossy finish that belied their low-budget origins and starring Lee and Cushing. Their competitor in the field Amicus was run by two producers, Max J. Rosenberg and Milton Subotsky.

Max looked after the marketing side, and the product was mostly handled by Milton. He had seen some of my television work and gave me my first chance, as he had done earlier for Dick Lester with a pop music movie called *It's Trad Dad*. When the script arrived from my agent and I read the title page, my heart sank. It was called *The House That Dripped Blood*. Milton Subotsky favoured the multiple story format and, like most of the company output, *The House That Dripped Blood* consisted of four episodes. They were taken from original tales by Robert Bloch, who had written the novel on which Hitchcock based his horror classic *Psycho*. All the stories were set in the same rather evil house where nasty fates awaited the various people foolish enough to rent it. Happily the script was rather good, nothing like as bad as its appalling title. Not a drop of blood was visible anywhere, in neither the script nor the movie that I subsequently made from it, and I felt I would have great fun shooting it. In any case, a movie was a movie, and who was I to turn it down? So I went to meet Milton Subotsky at Shepperton Studios where Amicus worked out of two prefabricated buildings on the back lot—characteristic, I think, of their low-budget profile. Milton was an extraordinary autodidact with a photographic memory. There was hardly a work of fiction you could mention that he hadn't read and remembered and of which he could give an assessment of its commercial possibilities. He liked to boast in print that Amicus made films cheap and fast, which was at least honest. Most film producers go the other way and inflate the budgets of their films in press handouts. Milton had a somewhat brash and socially uneasy personality which I think made him a few enemies in the business and, although we did not always agree on artistic matters, I got on very well with him. His partner Max Rosenberg suffered badly from halitosis and liked to talk of Amicus' work as being a "two-tier operation." What I think he meant was that on the one hand they made serious artistic films of quality and, on the other the trashy commercial stuff like their horror movies. I was duly signed up to make this particular piece of trash. The two big stars of the genre, Christopher Lee (now Sir Christopher) and Peter Cushing, had already accepted leading roles in two of the stories and therefore finance was assured.

One of the great difficulties for a director on a low-budget omnibus-type movie is that going over schedule even for half a day on any one story causes a potentially disastrous domino effect. You have to get through at any cost because the actors on call for the next episode will turn up on time. So there was a great pressure to get through on schedule. If you didn't get it in the can then you would have a hole in the movie. It was as simple as that.

I worked on the script very hard for some weeks before I was actually even on the payroll, planning how I would shoot the film and discussing with the production designer Tony Curtis how we would give the film as glossy a look as was possible given the time schedule and budgetary restrictions. For the exterior of the dreaded house we were to use an old unused building on the Shepperton lot which had been a lodge at the gates in the days before the estate became a film studio. Tony added a few details to give it the right sort of Gothic/Norman Bates look for those scenes where the estate agent—whose name was Stoker! —brought the prospective tenants to view the property. For the interior I wanted a sombre look in greys and greens with no hint of bright primary colours and above all I needed a staircase so that I could play the action on two levels when it was dramatically effective. Tony also ransacked the studio property stores and produced a phantasmagoria of baroque furnishings, decorated lecterns, pieces of statuary, and old bookcases that would be stuffed with books on horror and the occult borrowed from Milton's own extensive library, plus one or two books on horror movies from my own shelves. All this provided opportunities for evocative camera set-ups.

In the first episode called "Method for Murder," the house is rented by Charles Hillyer, a writer of horror stories who becomes obsessed with one of his own characters called Dominick, who then turns into a frightening reality. This creation, which bore an intentional resemblance to Boris Karloff's monster in *Frankenstein*, appears from time to time in various corners of the house or peering through the bushes outside the window when the author sits at his typewriter developing his story. At one point I had Charles alone in the dark living room, looking into a mirror over the fireplace and seeing the staircase reflected with Dominick's face in the shadows at the top of the stairs. When Charles turns around to look, nobody is visible, so he begins to climb the staircase to have a look. This, of course, follows one of the conventions of the horror genre. The hero or heroine always has to advance into the realm of the evil forces, be it at the top of the stairs or into the dark wood or wherever, when in real life he or she would just get the hell out of it! It is all about working on the fears of the audience. Our instinct is to shout "Don't do it!" We know that Count Dracula or Frankenstein's monster or the Wolf Man or some demented killer like dear old Norman in *Psycho* is there waiting in the dark.

I was lucky and pleased to get Denholm Elliott to play Charles, the writer, which he did with great subtlety and believability. Not for one moment was there any hint in his performance that this role was any less serious a challenge than the major and much more important ones that one had seen him play so outstandingly in major films over the years. Although I met him socially quite often, before and after the movie, I could not claim him as a close friend, but like everybody else in the business, I was saddened by his tragic early death.

I added a little black humour in the episode. While viewing the house with his wife, played by Joanna Dunham, and being fascinated by the way it mirrored the subject matter of his stories, the writer notices a skull on the desk in the study. He tips it back to open the mouth and reveal an ink-well inside. I gave Denholm a throw away line: Hamlet's famous "Alas poor Yorick." Milton enthusiastically agreed to the line and added his own suggestion. "Yeah, great idea," he said. "Why don't we say, 'Alas poor Yorick. I knew him ink well'?" I winced. "Well, er, yes, Milton," I replied. "Let's see how it plays." All I shot was my original suggestion, but unbelievably the line was cut in the editing on the basis that an audience would not know the reference, which seemed a pretty patronising attitude. In any case, I argued, those who don't know it wouldn't notice it while those who did would find it moderately amusing—and as it only takes one or two seconds to say, why cut it out? It's one of the most famous quotes in the whole of literature and anyone who is the least bit literate knows it. This was a minor irritation at the time, and I don't remember who raised the objection, but I suspect it was Rosenberg.

After Denholm had come to a sticky end at the hands of Dominick, who turned out to be his wife's lover in disguise, the house was then rented by a retired City stockbroker Philip Grayson played by Peter Cushing. Grayson is lost in the memories of a woman he had loved but not won. This story was a variation on that old standby of the genre, the Wax Museum. Visiting it by chance, Grayson

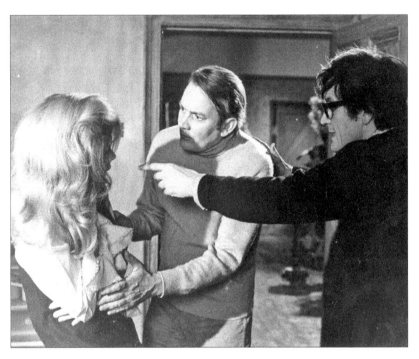

A dramatic moment between Denholm Elliott and Joanna Dunham.

becomes obsessed with the wax figure of Salome holding the head of John the Baptist on a plate, for it reminds him of his long lost love.

As one might expect, the whole thrust of the story was that Peter Cushing's head was going to end up on that plate, too, thanks to the mad axe-man who ran the museum, played by Wolfe Morris in fine sinister form. Joss Ackland played a friend and old rival for the affections of the lost love, whose head also ends up on Salome's plate during the course of the action.

To give the story some resonance, I built up the loneli-

With Peter Cushing and Ray Parslow, cinema photographer.

ness of the Cushing character as he walked around the village and lingered on a riverbank, in a scene that was inspired by the German Romantic painter, Caspar David Frederich. Sitting alone in the house, brooding over remembrance of things past, he listens to Schubert's melancholy string quartet *Death and the Maiden* while leafing through souvenirs of past happy moments. I brought to the studio some old theatre programmes for this scene and offered them to Peter. He shuffled through them and picked out a few, including one of Laurence Olivier and Vivien Leigh in the Royal Shakespeare production of Rich-

The River Bank - discussing German Romantic painting with Peter Cushing - not too pretentiously I hope.

ard Sheridan's *The School For Scandal.* He reminded me that he had played Sir Joseph Surface in that very production, which made a nice little in-reference.

Peter was a gentle, quiet and charming man and a pleasure to work with. At the time we made the film his wife Helen was seriously ill, but I felt that it would be intrusive of me, who had only just met him, to ask about it, and only later did I get to know that she was, in fact, terminally ill. I am sure that the sadness of what was happening in his personal life was mirrored in the sensitive performance he gave in my film.

This was, sadly, the one story in the movie where its low budget origins really showed. The wax heads of Peter, Joss and the Salome figure herself were awful beyond belief, and this made the moment when Peter first sees her (and is supposed to be struck by her strange resemblance to his lost love) not only unbelievable but also quite laughable. When these shoddy efforts were offered up for my inspection on the set, it was far too late to have anything done about them, and so I had to grin and bear it. In any case, it was a forlorn hope that Amicus would have spent the money for some decent ones in the first place.

The third story starred Christopher Lee as John Reid, the father of Jane, an innocent-looking little girl who turns out to be a witch and who burns her father in effigy by throwing a waxen image of him into the sitting room fire.

I cast an extraordinarily angelic-looking little child named Chloe Franks who played her role with an eerie kind of self-assurance. Christopher is a tall man and a dominating presence on the screen in whatever he plays. My opening scene of their story had Christopher looking around the living room of the house when he calls the child in from outside the front door. Little Chloe calmly entered the room and immediately commanded the audience's attention as she drifted almost fairy-like around the room. At the rushes next day, Christopher sighed. "They are quite right," he said wryly. "Never play with children or animals." Later in the story, he sits quietly reading, waiting for the

John Reid (Christopher Lee) realising he is the victim
of his daughter's frightening powers.

Christopher Lee and Nyree Dawn Porter.

new nanny Mrs. Norton, played by Nyree Dawn Porter, to arrive to look after his angelic little monster. He said he would like to use one of his favourite books, JRR Tolkien's *The Lord of the Rings*. Much more recently, of course, he played the evil *Saruman* in the Peter Jackson films, something that must have made him very pleased indeed.

I felt a need for an additional sequence to emphasise Jane's development as a witch. I invented a short scene in which Jane is taking a walk with her nanny and teacher and identifies the different kinds of trees they pass. After she correctly names a yew tree, she turns to her teacher and

Nyree Dawn Porter and Chloe Franks.

says, "You know something, Mrs.Norton. In olden days, yew trees used to be evil, magic trees." When I suggested the scene to Milton, he disagreed with me and said that it wouldn't do anything and I shouldn't waste time shooting it. When he wasn't looking, I got the unit out on the lot and we shot the scene in double-quick time. When Milton saw it in rushes, he had the grace to tell me I was right, and the scene is, of course, in the film.

Christopher Lee is an extraordinary man. He's full of what you might think of as Baron Munchausen stories about himself—but they all turn out to be true. He's had the most remarkable career. You can talk to him about almost any subject and he knows something about it. He is a man who, I think, perhaps because of his commanding height, may at first appearance seem formidable. In fact he is immensely endearing. He has a great passion for life and many passions within that general life, like his great love for opera. He's also a great singer. It's funny but he is the only man I've ever known who is able to describe a Mozart opera in terms of one of the basso supporting roles, which he can sing!

The last segment was a comedy piece about a low-budget Dracula movie in which the star, who is the next tenant of the house, ends up as a real vampire. The role of the self-opinionated, rather camp Paul Henderson was originally offered to Vincent Price, but he was not available, and the role was played instead by the British comedy actor Jon Pertwee. Playing opposite Jon as Carla, his co-star in the movie, was the Queen of Lady Vampires, Ingrid Pitt. From the moment they arrived to view the house in a large, open Rolls Royce, Jon and the voluptuous Ingrid, wearing a large floppy white hat and a décolleté blue dress and smoking a cigarette in a ridiculously long holder, played their roles with flamboyant style.

Having trashed the set and the costumes as not worthy of him or the genre, Paul Henderson buys another cloak that turns out to be a real vampire's cloak from a character named Von Hartman who runs a weird little antique shop.

Jon suggested to me that it would be fun if he actu-

Ingrid Pitt and Jon Pertwee.

Jon and I hamming it up

ally flew when he first tried on the cloak, with the clock striking twelve and fangs starting to appear in his mouth. I thought it was a great idea but expressed some concern about the stunt man's harness that he would have to wear. He said it would be no problem for him as he had flown on stage in pantomime at some point in his career.

Ingrid was game, too, which gives a splendid climax to the story when she admits to being a real vampire herself and saying "Welcome to the club!" flies up to the top landing to bury her fangs in the terrified actor's neck.

After this episode, it was really not possible to go back

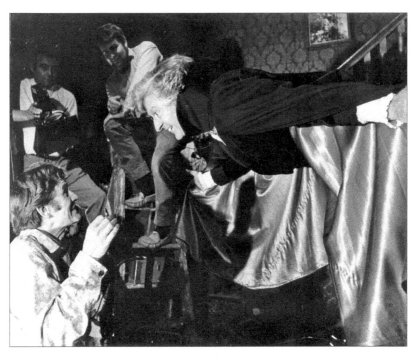

Jon Pertwee flying high.

to the straight horror style of the previous three stories. A Scotland Yard detective, played by John Bennett, who is investigating the disappearance of Paul Henderson now visits the house—at night of course—and encounters the resident vampires in the basement. I tried to pay a little jokey homage to German Expressionist cinema here. We had huge shadows on the wall as Jon Pertwee's vampire attacks the policeman, and I had intended to play the sequence against a silent movie-type piano track. The front office, of course, didn't get the joke and hacked the sequence down. They wanted it to be scarier, but by cutting it, they did not

The Queen of Vampires strikes again.

make it more serious, they just made it less funny.

Milton Subotsky was what we in the business call a "hands-on producer"—one who can't direct but thinks he can control the film in the cutting room. Many producers are like this: they won't actually put themselves on the line to direct the picture but take the director's material and cut it. I have to admit to a certain quiet little battle that would go on between Milton and me in the cutting room. But he was not too bad that way—he just had his ideas and stood up and argued them. Nowadays, if the film is big enough and commercially successful, like Ridley Scott's *Blade Runner*, for example, the producers then feel confident enough to squeeze a few more bucks out of the project by issuing the director's cut. This was not likely to be the case with *The House That Dripped Blood*.

I hated the title of the film and so did my actors. Max Rosenberg insisted on it. I went down on my bended knees—metaphorically, not literally—and pleaded, "Please don't call this picture *The House That Dripped Blood*." It's a cheap, vulgar exploitation title. I wanted to call it *Death and the Maiden* as I had used the Schubert String Quartet in the Peter Cushing episode and because each of the stories in its own way is about just that. But Rosenberg insisted that this was the marketplace title. Maybe he was right, but it's not a title I've ever been happy with. And it was a bit of an albatross around my neck for quite a time. Milton's next project, which he offered to me, was a version of Robert Louis Stevenson's *Dr. Jekyll and Mr. Hyde*. Milton had been reading an article in a scientific journal about the optics of the human eye, and from this he had gleaned that if each eye had a different optical characteristic and the image arrived at the eye at different times, then, somehow, a two-dimensional picture in movement could appear to have three dimensional qualities. This gave him the idea that one could make a cheap 3D movie. What was required was to wear in the cinema a pair of sunglasses with only one lens in place and to film with a constantly moving camera. I may have appeared a little skeptical, and Milton suggested that I try out his idea in the cinema. I dutifully did so and went to a local cinema to see Robert Redford in *Downhill Racer*, a film about a skiing champion that would certainly have abundant fast-moving camera movement in it. I found that although the 3D was sometimes effective, it was completely dependent on where you sat and how close you were to the screen, and you were likely to get a splitting headache. Neither did I like the idea of a constantly moving camera, which I felt was artistically quite wrong for the horror genre that often relied for its effect on static, wide-angle shots of atmospheric interiors like Dracula's castle and Frankenstein's laboratory and gloomy sinister landscapes. So I turned it down, as also did Freddie Francis.

Shortly after the film's release, I got my first fan letter:

Dear Sir/Madam

May I respectfully point out a small fault which I noticed when I went to see your film, "The House That Dripped Blood." At the beginning, which I must admit I thoroughly enjoyed, a policeman in uniform was talking to a plainclothes inspector in a police station. He said words to the effect that something strange happened in the house about two years ago. Then, as the film went on to show what happened the young couple they were talking about

*drove up a sports car that clearly by the
registration number was only one year-old
at the most. As the car was clearly in view,
this caught my eye immediately.*

*However, I am glad to say the rest of the
film made up for this fault, and I look
forward to seeing a film equal to this one.*

Yours respectfully,
Mr P Easton

I thought I might send Mr. Easton a reply complimenting him on spotting the deliberate mistake, but that seemed a little unkind, so I resisted the temptation.

Some thirty years later, I still get letters asking me about the movie and what it was like working with Peter and Christopher. *The House That Dripped Blood* has become a cult classic of the genre. More has been written about it than about any of the other, more serious films that I have made, and it often gets shown at horror film festivals. It is now released on DVD, which will give it another lease of life—or death. Christopher, in his first autobiography, *Tall Dark and Gruesome*, made some nice comments about me that I found flattering indeed and, happily, *The House that Dripped Blood* was not to be the last time that I worked with him.

A Note by Ingrid Pitt

Film directors come in two fragrances. And sometimes in a blend of the two. On the one hand you have the disciples of Alfred Hitchcock who believe that all actors are cattle to be fed into his trough. Dabbed behind the ears are the directors who acknowledge that the artistes come with their own talents and should be allowed to demonstrate it under their guidance. Peter Duffell, thankfully, comes in the latter category. When I was first approached about appearing in *The Cloak* I thought it was going to be another fangs and fetish oeuvre. It might have been if it wasn't for Peter. He, and Jon Pertwee, produced a nice little send-up of the genre without belittling it. And I can't remember him actually getting into the melee that surrounds the set and telling us how to do our job. A rare quality in a director and one that shows an enormous strength of character.

—Ingrid Pitt

A Journey to Greeneland

Monster was not the only Amicus film I turned down, although it was financially a tough decision to make. I had greatly enjoyed making *The House That Dripped Blood*, but I did not want to become typecast as a horror movie director, so I also said no to another film that Milton offered me called *Tales from the Crypt*.

Then, in the early 1970s, thanks to a recommendation from Jan Read who was story editor on *Man in a Suitcase*, I was approached by an American producer, Jack Levin, to direct a film based on the novel *England Made Me* by Graham Greene. The underlying story was one of an incestuous relationship between twins Anthony and Kate Farrant set against a larger backlog of political financial skullduggery in Sweden in the 1930s. I had read it many years before, but rereading it, I realized how, like most of Greene's novels, it stayed in the mind. I met Jack Levin in London and was given a copy of the script that had been written by the well-known English writer, Wolf Mankowitz. I thought it was a terrible travesty of Greene's novel.

The background of the story had been transformed into some sort of swinging '60s Sweden with all the sexual permissiveness implied by the time and place in the popular imagination. The script ended with brother and sister making love on a boat during a midsummer night party. This completely and vulgarly distorted the central theme of the novel, which was that Anthony and Kate both avoided the essential truth of their relationship. One fact I was certain about was that if I were going to direct the movie, I was certainly not going to make this script. But I thought I would deal with that problem later so, keeping my peace on the issue for the moment, I accepted and a deal was made by my agent.

This was a time when, looking for cheap places to make movies, many film companies set up productions in Yugoslavia where attractive deals could be made with the state film studios anxious to do business with the West. Wartime action stories like *The Dirty Dozen* were shot there. Mel Brooks was one of the first to explore the possibilities of shooting cheaply in central Europe with a comedy called *The Twelve Chairs,* starring Ron Moody. He seems to have had a somewhat unhappy time there, for a joke was going around the industry that he had invented something called "Yugoslavs Anonymous," the purpose of which was to help anybody who wanted to make a movie in that country.

Before I came on board, Jack Levin had already made

some preliminary plans to shoot the film in Yugoslavia. So I went there on a location reconnaissance trip with a production manager to explore the potential. I was still not certain how I was going to realize the novel, but I had various vague ideas knocking around in my head. We met some people from Yugo-Slav government film studios, and they showed me places where they thought we could film. We needed a big villa and were shown just the place at beautiful Lake Bled in Slovenia. Then we saw Opatija on the Adriatic Coast, which I thought was potentially an interesting location and, of course, there was Belgrade itself. It suffered heavily during the war from German bomber raids, and much of it had been rebuilt in a functional and rather character-less style, but parts of the city still reflected the country's long domination by the Austrian Hapsburg Empire. I am sure that at this time the Yugoslavs must have felt that I was slightly crazy or just worryingly indecisive, because nothing I said or asked of them had anything to do with that which they had already seen.

Happily, on my return, I was able to persuade Jack Levin that the script needed much work. I went to see Wolf Mankowitz, who was now ensconced as a tax exile in Dublin. He was pleasant, but quite adamant that he had no intention of doing any further work on the script, which suited me fine. I contracted an old university friend of mine, Shaun McCarthy, who, under his nom-de-plume Desmond Cory, had written a number of successful thrillers including *Dead Fall*, which Bryan Forbes had filmed with Michael Caine. I told Shaun that I was in trouble, I needed a new script, I didn't think I had time to do it alone and I desperately needed someone to bounce ideas off. Sean said he was game, and we set to work. Our guiding principle was that we do our best to remain faithful to Graham Greene's story and his intentions as we understood them. It's the concrete nature of his work that can make the task seem deceptively easy. His writing style used a kind of cinematic montage technique that you can bring to the screen, and you can take your cue from that. We used certain techniques in the film that were inspired by his own method in the novels, the pointing towards certain objects in a *mise-en-scene* to give a feeling of place. In a way, that was the easiest part, but it is a deceptive easiness because what his stories are about in essence is the human condition, about betrayal and guilt, the evils of the world we live in and our failure to survive honorably. The externals are easy to put on the screen, but they are what you might call—to use T.S.Eliot's famous phrase— "an objective correlative" for the internal emotions and feelings inside the characters.

Shaun suggested we changed the setting to Nazi Germany. It would work, he argued, and perhaps give the piece more meaning for a contemporary audience. I was a bit reluctant at first, but neither of us knew anything much about Sweden in the thirties, although we knew a fair amount about Germany in the same period. Also, we saw a clue to it from Greene himself in his introduction to the novel, where he wrote that the thirties were overshadowed by the rise of Nazism in Germany and the depression in England. I felt that I could possibly recreate Nazi Germany in Yugoslavia, but certainly I could not recreate Sweden there.

So we set to work and produced a new script in about three weeks, which was all the time at our disposal. We were faced with the problem of explaining the relationship between the two main characters Tony Farrant and his stronger sister Kate, and this is defined by certain actions which have taken place in the past which make clear the way both of them behave at key moments in the story. The influence that Kate has over her rather ne'er-do-well brother and her strength of character are defined by one incident during their school days: Anthony decides to run away from school and meets his sister in a deserted barn at night and she firmly orders him to go back to school. In the novel, this is talked about by Tony and Kate in their first meeting. If this was left as no more than a long verbal explanation by the actors it would be very static and could only be taken in by the audience in words and not pictures. If sensitively handled the flashback can go a long way to solve this problem, for a character's actions and his motivations can be more clearly understood by the use of this technique. But there are other possible solutions. Our solution to dealing with it in film terms was to shoot it as a pre-credit sequence rather than simply have the grown-up pair refer to it in dialogue.

We now had a script that I would not be ashamed to offer to leading actors. The next challenge was casting. First and most important was the role of Tony Farrant, the charming, young English ne'er-do-well who bounced out of one job to another failure, to the despair of his loving twin sister who was as ambitious and driven as he was happy-go-lucky. After one or two false starts, I had lunch with Michael York and his wife Patricia. Michael, whom I felt sure was absolutely right casting, was charming but a little hesitant about accepting the role. He had just finished shooting *Cabaret* in which he played a young Englishman in Berlin, and he did not want to repeat himself. When we said goodbye after a pleasant lunch, I felt that I had not convinced him. I was over the moon when his agent rang to say that Michael had had second thoughts and would be happy to do my picture. Then I approached Susannah York (no relation to Michael) to play his sister, Kate Farrant, which would have been interesting casting. Real twins had usually been disastrous in movies, and for this reason we had made an earlier decision to leave out this aspect of the brother and sister relationship, but Michael and Susannah could have been believable twins and, oddly enough, had the same name. However, she had accepted a Robert Altman picture, which ruled her

Michael York and Hildegard Neil as Tony and Kate Farrant.

out, and we then approached Hildegard Neil, whose work on television had impressed me.

The third important character in the novel was Krogh, the international financier based on the notorious Ivan Kruger, the "Swedish match king" who was at the centre of a financial scandal at the time. I had visualized him as a rather coarse version of Charles Foster "Citizen" Kane, and I felt that Joss Ackland, who worked with me on the Peter Cushing episode of my horror movie, would be good casting. I took Jack Levin with me to see Joss on stage—he was appearing in Shaw's *Captain Brassbound's Conversion* opposite Ingrid Bergman. But Jack felt that Joss was not a bankable enough name to carry the film.

It was then that Peter Finch's agent approached me and asked if we would be interested. Of course we were, and an offer was made. I had met Peter some years before that, but not in connection with movies. He was living in a flat off the Fulham Road and dined regularly at a Spanish Restaurant there called Casa Pepe. This was at that time when I was deeply into flamenco music. I often sat in with the "cuadro" at Casa Pepe, and it was then I first met Peter, who was enamored of a Spanish dancer in the troupe who performed there nightly. Sometimes after the restaurant closed, we would go round to Peter's flat that he shared with his friend, Vincent Ball, another Australian actor. I don't think Peter had much luck with Salud, the girl in question, who was a well-brought-up young lady from a Catholic Gibraltarian background, but his pursuit provided the alarming spectacle of Finchie, after a few too many glasses of vino, attempting to dance a *farruca* with her on the Casa Pepe dance floor. One evening the group came up to a party at my house in Hampstead and brought Peter with them, but I think he was too inebriated to remember the event, for he had to be taken home in a taxi shortly after he arrived. Little did I know at that time that one day I would be working with him in Yugoslavia.

In the world of independent film production, you can not be sure that a film will become a reality until the day that filming actually starts, and sometimes, even after that, the situation can be so financially rocky that life be-

Peter Finch as Erich Krogh.

comes a day-by-day struggle for existence. I invited Peter for dinner to discuss the film and he asked me outright if it was a real "goer." I said firmly, with one hand behind my back with fingers crossed, that it certainly was. Joss then rang me up and asked me if I would consider him to play Krogh's villainous henchman. Surprised but delighted, I said okay. A young actress, Tessa Wyatt, was cast to play the gauche young English girl on holiday in Germany who was picked up and seduced by Tony Farrant. Michael Sheard was set to play the Jewish newspaper owner, Fromm. That left one other major role, the seedy old Etonian journalist, Minty. My first thought was Denholm Elliot, who had been so good in my horror movie, but Denholm was busy. Suddenly staring at me from the pages of *Spotlight* was Michael Hordern, and I wondered why I had been stupid and not shortlisted him before. To my delight, Michael said yes and we were now ready to go so far as our casting was concerned.

We started our filming with many scenes on Lake Bled where Michael York as Tony Farrant rowed his sister Kate across the lake to the great villa owned by her lover, the financier Krogh. When you are filming in a studio, you see each day the "rushes," or "dailies" as the Americans call them, of the work you have done the day before. So early in the morning before shooting starts for the day, or sometimes at lunchtime, all the key technicians and heads of departments, the producer and the director sit

Michael Hordern as Minty.

in a viewing theatre and look at the results of the previous day's work, judge the quality of the lighting and camera work, set design, make-up, and a host of other technical problems. All of these elements are the concern of the director, of course, but he also has to judge the actors' performances. Are they giving the interpretation that is in his mind, and has he designed good camera angles and movements for what he is trying to express? Rushes can cause high anxiety for every member of the crew, but ultimately the director has overall responsibility for what is on the screen.

In pre-digital days, one of the problems of shooting on location, particularly in a foreign country, was that it was well nigh impossible to see rushes daily. Usually the negative was sent home for an English laboratory to process, and then the editor had to combine the sound tracks with the picture for the rushes' showing. This could mean that nothing would be seen by the film makers for maybe a week. Often no cinema was available so that the material had to be shown on a mobile projector in the hotel, or at worst on a video with a VHS "lifted" from the print. This was particularly agonizing for the first week of filming because it meant that you were flying blind. This was the case with *England Made Me*, and it was a week later before my editor, Malcolm Cooke, turned up with the cans of film so anxiously awaited by all of us. We had been blessed with the most wonderful autumnal weather, and the light on the water was quite extraordinary. I felt happy and confident as I sat with the crew, some members of the cast and the producer and his wife, looking at the results of our first week's work. Ray Parslow, my cinematographer who had worked with me on *The House that Dripped Blood*, had done a beautiful job, the actors were clearly comfortable in their roles and the costumes looked great. But when the lights went up at the end, the producer walked out without saying a word. After that, despite my own praise for their work, my crew walked out of the room completely deflated.

I retired to my room to prepare for the next day's schedule, and it was only later that I heard that Finchie—God bless him—had rounded on Jack in the hotel bar and loudly castigated him with the odd four letter word for not showing any enthusiasm for what he had seen. Much later, when we were recording the music in Olympic Studios in Barnes, Jack's wife confessed to me that they had been alarmed because the story was not unwinding coherently on the screen but seemed all chopped up in bits and pieces, which, of course, it was. It was Jack's first time out as a producer: he was a complete beginner with little understanding at that time of how movies were actually made. He was completely incapable of reading rushes. Hence his worry because what I was doing seemed to him to make no sense at all. It was obvious that Finchie's outburst still caused them embarrassment.

Peter was a consummate screen actor, and working with him was immensely satisfying. He was always word perfect when the camera started to roll, and for him the first take was always the best. The second take, he would say to me, would be okay, but by the fourth he would be going downhill and, because he believed this, it was usually the case. This did present me with a tricky problem earlier in the filming because Hildegarde needed several takes before getting her performance right, but she quickly got over what was probably largely nerves and lack of confidence. Film, as the old cliché has it, is a visual medium telling its story in pictures. Finchie would often come to me at the beginning of the day's filming to discuss his dialogue. "Look Peter," he would say, "this speech—the first sentence okay, the second sentence I don't need to say that. I can act it." He was usually right, and I was more than happy to cut the lines in question. Looking back, I am pretty sure that they were lines added by Shaun and myself, for Graham's dialogue was always marvelously economical and easy for actors to speak. Michael, on the other hand, would come to me with a copy of the novel and point out when we had missed a good line of dialogue in the original.

The mark of a good screen actor is to be found in the close-up shot. You can always cut to it, even when you had not planned to do so, because the actor is always expressing something, however subtle it may be. In other words, he or she never stops reacting to the drama that is unfolding. Both Finchie and York were exceptional in this respect.

As an undergraduate I had seen Finchie on stage playing Iago to Orson Welles' *Othello*, which the great man directed himself at the old St. James' Theatre, and I had reviewed it for *Isis*, the University student's magazine. I mentioned this to Peter one day while we were shooting, and he told me a couple of stories about that experience. Orson, he said, had approved a dark brown costume for him, and he tended to place him in shadow on the stage whenever possible. The production ran over a Christmas period, and Welles had a Christmas card designed that showed the outside of the theatre with a billboard, in front of which he had a pile of snow so that it showed only his own name and covered that of Peter Finch and other members of the cast. Other stories about Welles at that time passed into legend. For example, his anger was considerable at Ken Tynan's review of the production in *The Observer*, in which Tynan referred to him as Citizen Coon and said that he rose to the heights of his limitations as an actor. Orson got his own back when Tynan arrived at his dressing room on one occasion, and Welles pretended to believe that he was an actor looking for work. He bluntly told him that with his stammer he could have no future on the boards. Then there was the occasion when during one scene in the play, Orson managed to hit hard and painfully Maxine Audley (who played Desdemona's servant and Iago's wife Emilia) and during the final curtain calls, whenever the curtain came down on the actors standing hand-in-hand smiling and bowing at the audience, Maxine would give Orson a hefty clout in retaliation, both of them having to regain their composure as the curtain rose again. Maxine worked with me on one of my Scotland Yarders, and I asked her if this story were true. She answered that it certainly was.

Peter also took over the leading male role from Dirk Bogarde in Jean Anouilh's play, *Point of Departure*, with Mai Zetterling. He told me that one night the Queen Mother Mary, widow of King George V, came to see the play and, during the interval, he and Mai Zetterling were commanded to visit the Royal Box. The august Royal lady looked at the two of them and complimented Mai Zetterling on her performance, which she said was very good. Then she turned to Peter and said "And you, young man - very bad!"

When filming was completed in Yugoslavia, it was back to the UK to shoot the opening pre-credit sequence of the boy Tony running away from the school he hates so much and meeting his sister Kate at night in a barn where she persuades him to return. I had cast two young actors, Richard Gibson and Lalla Ward who later starred in the famous television series *Dr Who*, to play the roles and, as well as looking reasonably like a young Michael York and Hildegard Neil, they played the scene with great sensitivity, Several times in the film, I was able to create

With Peter Finch and Joss Ackland outside the Nazi headquarters.

a visual metaphor for Kate's power over Tony by placing her above him, first in the barn where she looks down on him from the hay loft and later from the top of the ornate staircase outside Krogh's apartment where he has a momentary image of her as the schoolgirl in the barn. I was also able to use the same idea in scenes at Krogh's palatial villa. At Pinewood studios, I shot a few necessary inserts for the party scene at the villa, using tried and tested professional actors. Then it was into the cutting rooms and the recording studios with the composer John Scott who produced a lovely film score.

One basic axiom of the film industry is that you never start a film unless you have a distribution guarantee—and you certainly don't finance it with your own money. Although Jack had raised his finance from a sound source (the Wall Street financier, Bob Allen), we had no distribution lined up before shooting. When the film was finished and Jack was in New York, it fell to me to deliver a print for consideration by Arthur Abeles, at that time the head of Warner Bros. in London. I waited a couple of nail-biting days and then rang the Warner offices. At first I seemed to be getting the polite stalling technique, Mr. Abeles was in conference, etc., etc., but then my hopes rose as his secretary told me he would actually speak to me. When he came on the line, his first words were that he thought the picture looked like four million dollars on the screen (a lot of money in those days) although he knew it had cost only about a million. My hopes were raised even further. Then they came crashing to the ground. "But," he added, "we pass." The dreaded word "pass" is the polite way of saying "no deal" in the film business. Finally Jack did make a deal with the English distribution company formed by the actor David Hemmings and John Daly, Hemdale, and a date was set for the London premiere.

Just before that, Graham Greene was in London, and

the film was run for him in a Wardour Street viewing theatre. He turned up with his wife Vivienne, to whom the
book was dedicated and from whom he had been separated for many years. I was introduced to them by Jack
Levin and then, I must confess, my courage failed me and
I fled, fearing that he might hate the film. A few days later
I got a short note from him from his home in Antibes in the
South of France saying he was "pleased enough." That
was certainly good enough for me, knowing how often
he had disliked the films made from his work and that
he had not scripted himself. The London premiere was a

Waiting for the stars to arrive at The London Premiere.

fairly grand affair at the Odeon Theatre in Shaftesbury Avenue, even featuring some trumpeters from a Household Regiment who were commonly hired for this kind of gig.

Then came the reviews. They were on the whole very good indeed, particularly those from the critics of the serious broad sheets. First of them was Alexander Walker in the *London Evening Standard*: "*England Made Me* exists in its own right as very much a film to be seen," he wrote. "One of those rare films that have a tone of their own, know where they're going and get there and take you with them all the way." Gavin Millar, writing at that time for one of the national newspapers, was particularly kind and said that he thought the transition to Nazi Germany gave us handy signposts. Philip Strick in the BFI journal, *Sight and Sound*, wrote a long and enthusiastic article, at the end of which he commented that this film should be the making of its director. The lady who wrote for the posh and trendy monthly *Vogue* found the film not at all to her taste, however.

When a French distribution deal was set up, there was a Paris premiere in the Theatre Champs d'Elyseés. We all went to Paris for a couple of days, including Peter Finch and Michael York, who was also there for the opening of Dick Lester's *Three Musketeers* in which he played d'Artagnan. We put Peter up at L'Hotel on the South Bank, which had been the last home for Oscar Wilde and was now transformed into a *très chic* establishment. I felt this was appropriate as Peter had earlier given a memorable performance as the great Oscar in Ken Hughes' film and, when we were shooting in Yugoslavia, this was the film that all the local film buffs had eagerly asked him about. Our title was not a good one for the French, and they re-titled the film *Le Financier,* which was at least adequate. But there remained the all-important problem of an American pickup. Finally Jack negotiated a deal with a small New York distribution company whose catalogue of properties filled me with some foreboding, but at least we were going to get the film seen across the other side of the Atlantic, and I arrived in New York for the opening at the Plaza Cinema. The N.Y. reviews were a mixed bag but on the whole pretty good. Judith Crist was enthusiastic in the columns of *The New Yorker*, and the reviewer in Andy Warhol's magazine was also full of praise. Andy Warhol himself turned up for the opening. However, the all-powerful Vincent Canby of *The New York Times* slaughtered us. We had, he wrote, the presumption to change the *mise-en-scene* from Sweden to Germany and the film was thoroughly bad in all respects. Canby, they said, could make or break a movie, and if this were true, then he certainly broke us, for the film failed commercially in the States and did my career no immediate good at all. The distinguished Pauline Kael of the *New Yorker* was critical but rather nice about the film, and she wrote complimentary comments about my handling of the actors and the quality of the dialogue. As she was notoriously dismissive of European films as a whole (my friend John Schlesinger had nick-named her "Pauline Cruel" after she had attacked one of his movies), I felt I got away pretty lightly. She had written of what she saw as over-precious design in the colour of a frock worn by Hildegard that strikingly matched the clear translucent blue of the lake behind her. I spoke to Miss Kael on the phone to thank her for what was on the whole a good review, and I pointed out that the colour match was purely accidental. "Oh," she said.

I soon learned that if critic A liked the movie, then pretty certainly critic B who was known not to like critic A would not like the film. This was particularly true in the case of Pauline Kael and *Village Voice* critic Andrew Sarris, who didn't like it. Kael had savaged Sarris in a long attack on *auteur* theory in the pages of the magazine. Also, a leading Canadian critic whose work was widely published didn't like the film, either, but Michael had warned me of this because said critic had apparently made a pass at Michael some time in the past—at a film festival, I be-lieve—and had not forgiven him for the rejection. He made scathing comments about what he called Michael's "Buster Brown" suits in the film. Somebody also told me that if *Time* magazine liked it, then *Newsweek* wouldn't, and this turned out to be true as well.

At that time I was naive enough to write replies to various critics who had slated us. Dear old George Melly, who was then film reviewer for the *Observer*, made a mild criticism that I had put in some heavy-handed period detail, referring to a packet of Gold Flake cigarettes and a film magazine on the bedside table in Tony Farrant's hotel room. I wrote to George pointing out the lines in the novel that indicated Tony's reading tastes and asked him what the hell he thought I should have him reading— James Joyce's *Ulysses* perhaps? But this was just friendly sparring as I knew George a little anyway.

But Canby who had written of our presumption had really stung me. I wrote an angry reply to the *New York Times* suggesting that as Graham Greene himself liked the movie, who then was the truly presumptuous one? Later I realized that answering critics was a fairly pointless exercise, for if you proved their assumptions wrong, they were not going to devote any space to admitting error, and if they didn't like your movie, they were fully entitled to say so and why. The only point to remember is that you cannot win them all.

The Ones That Got Away

They say a film director is only as good as his last picture, which really means that he's as good as the money it makes. In spite of a host of good reviews in England and the States, *England Made Me* was not a commercial success. Finance, as usual, was in short supply and I not only had to sell my house and move into a more modest place, but also, for a while, I was back to television series: *Black Beauty*, a tried and tested old film subject that Sidney Cole was producing, followed by a perfectly ghastly series based on Enid Blyton's *Famous Five* stories, which I have done my best to forget.

It is amazing how often horses seem to have featured in my work although I have only once in my life actually ridden one. After *Black Beauty*, it was equines again with a TV series produced by Jacky Stoller for Yorkshire Television: *The Racing Game* was based on the immensely popular mystery novels built around the horse racing scene, written by Dick Francis, one time jump-jockey. One of his most famous characters is Sid Halley, an ex-jockey who, after losing a hand in a racing accident, turns private investigator. The role was played by a Royal Shakespeare Company actor, Mike Gwilym and his side kick Chico Barnes by Mick Ford. One episode called "Gambling Lady" starred Caroline Blakiston as a woman obsessed with betting on horses, and, as her long-suffering Italian husband, Count Guiccoli, the film star matinee idol Anthony Steel, onetime husband of Anita Ekberg.

It was a complicated story involving the death of a horse which looked like an accident but was cold-bloodedly arranged by the villains of the piece. They lie about the dead horse's name, pretending he was a champion favorite, and claim a big insurance payout. Sid Halley is called in to investigate the claim and finds out that they were racing the champion using the name of the dead horse, which was a rank outsider with very long odds so they could clean up by putting a great deal of money on him. Part of the story was set at the Count's villa in Milan and this gave me the problem of finding a building somewhere near the studios in Leeds which would pass architecturally as an Italian Renaissance villa. By luck, we discovered at Ilkley, very near to Leeds, a large house in what was described as English Renaissance style designed by the famous Sir Edwin Lutyens. It worked perfectly and we were also able to make the road up to the villa look passably Italian by the judicious use of one or two props and extras, including one dressed as an Italian postman.

Anthony Steel was charm itself and, like the true English gentleman he was, showed no bitterness or resentment at the fact that he was no longer a box office star but was playing a supporting role in a TV series. We were having dinner together one evening in the hotel restaurant when he noticed that sitting at a nearby table was the distinguished actor Harry Andrews, who was appearing in a play in a Leeds theatre. He expressed his great admiration for Andrews' work at the Royal Shakespeare Company and, rather like a star-struck schoolboy, got up from our table, and went over to Harry Andrews to pay his respects. I felt rather touched by his humility and the obvious pleasure he derived from the encounter.

About this time, a line producer friend of mine offered me a script for a soft porno movie about artificial insemination. He sent it to me to read and said it could be made under a pseudonym so nobody would know I had directed it. I could take the money and run. I read the script. It was pretty awful, and I felt that even if I wanted to take it on, I couldn't shoot that sort of stuff anyway. In any event, the chap who did do it found his real name in brackets after the pseudonym in the British Film Institute bulletin review. So much for invisibility.

Every film director has on a shelf a pile of scripts and treatments that never got made, usually subjects that he felt passionately about and spent time and energy working on with no success. I have my fair share of those. After *England Made Me*, I was commissioned to write scripts for one or two projects that never reached the screen. I met Sam Arkoff, a cheerful buccaneer who ran American International, a low budget production house behind Roger Corman's horror movies and specializing in the genre. Classy literary adaptations were hardly the usual product for AIP but I was meeting Arkoff to discuss a projected version of *Camille*. I met Sam several times in a large apartment in the Savoy Hotel that he used on his visits to England. It transpired that Franco Zeffirelli was planning a *Camille* movie as well. What Sam was after was pipping him to the post and getting an AIP movie out first. A script was on the table and, as so often the case, it needed a total rewrite. I suggested to Arkoff that, because the events in the life of Marie Duplessis—the real *grande horizontale* who had inspired Alexander Dumas' novel—happened around the 1830s when a major revolution took place in France, and the French King was yet again deposed, we should set our story firmly against that background. He agreed in principle, so I went off to France for a few weeks and produced a draft script, in which I relied fairly heavily on the work of the great French novelists of the time, including Flaubert and Balzac. The result for Sam Arkoff was either too expensive or too arty or both, and I was asked if I would like to direct the original script if it ever happened at all. I said no and that was the end of that.

In the splendid C.S.Forester novel, *Death to the French*, a Rifle Brigade veteran of Wellington's Army in the Spanish Peninsula who is trapped behind the French lines fights a guerrilla war against Napoleon's occupying forces. I thought it would make a superb action adventure movie, and I had read a great deal about the Napoleonic period, which I had always found a fascinating era in European history. With some financial backing from The National Film Finance Corporation (a government body that existed at the time to encourage British film production), I bought an option on the book, traveled the battlefields of Portugal where the story was set, and produced a script. As usual this was offered to various leading actors, including Sean Connery, whose agent wrote to me to say in effect that if a film was set up and his fee agreed with a start date set, then he might just consider it. In other words, he was not prepared for me to float the picture on a commitment from him. Then came another fine actor, Robert Shaw, whom I had met once when he was "spear-carrying" with the Royal Shakespeare Company at Stratford-on-Avon in the days before he became a big star. Shaw read the script and showed great interest, but sadly he died of a heart attack shortly after, so I was back to square one. Various producers showed interest in the project, but nothing came of it. Much later, of course, a television series was made, built around Bernard Cornwell's novels about a Rifle Brigade soldier, the hero, Lieutenant Sharpe, played by Sean Bean. Perhaps I was just there at the wrong time.

A thriller called *The Crystal Contract* by Julian Rathbone I felt had great potential as a television series. I took out an option on the book and flew over to Los Angeles to discuss it with George Peppard, who had expressed interest in the project. We met in the Beverly Hills Hotel over lunch, and George, to my delight, wrote me a check on the spot to confirm his commitment. I returned home and wrote the first two scripts of the proposed series, which George liked very much. Then tragically, after he visited London to do a two-hander stage play with Elaine Stritch, he died from cancer. Once again, the Grim Reaper ended another project.

Then I read Graham Greene's latest book, *The Honorary Consul.* I liked it much indeed and summoned up the courage to write to Greene asking him if I might have a go at writing a screenplay. I was thrilled when I got a short letter from him saying yes. I wrote back to say that I would like to come down to the South of France where he had lived for many years and talk to him about the subject. I got a message back via his secretary who worked at the publishers, Bodley Head, saying, yes, by all means, and Mr. Greene would book me into a hotel. He had asked if I wanted something posh and classy or would I want something modestly shabby. An impecunious film director as opposed to a high-flying wheeler-dealer producer, I opted for the latter, and a week or two later found myself nervously ringing the bell of his flat at the Residence

With Graham Greene in Antibes.

des Fleurs in Antibes. The man himself, who, of course, I had met only for a brief moment at the Wardour Street showing of *England Made Me*, opened the door. He was a tall, slightly stooping figure with those penetrating blue eyes so frequently mentioned by people who had met him. The flat that I subsequently got to know fairly well was simple and functional. The living room lined with books had a small terrace that overlooked the harbour. Graham was supposed to be a difficult person to get on with, but he put me at my ease immediately and took me to the hotel in the town square where he had booked me a room. Then we dined together in a nearby restaurant. The poet W.B.Yeats wrote a wry little poem asking how, with that pretty girl nearby, could he concentrate on important things like politics? I, for my part, could in this situation pay attention only to the Master, but he, on the other hand, did not fail to notice and comment on a pretty girl sitting at a table across the room from us.

This was an important few days for me. After all, I had to convince a famous writer that I could write a decent screenplay based on one of his major books. I think we talked about literature a great deal—and movies a little. I probably recounted some of the problems associated with filming *England Made Me* and, naturally, we talked about *The Honorary Consul*. I said that I had read somewhere in his work that taking Cobbet's *Rural Rides* and various other books with him on one of his journeys probably robbed him of an opportunity to read *War and Peace* and that this had remained in my mind. The reason was, although I didn't say it, that if a great writer hadn't read it then I didn't have to feel guilty about not having read it, either. Graham said that he could not remember where he had said that. On the plane home I found out where. It was in his travel book, *The Lawless Roads*, about his trip to Mexico, which I had taken to read on the journey. I returned to England full of excitement and, as it turned out, he generously gave me a free option on the book for a year. With the help of a little pre-production money arranged by my agent that helped to keep me afloat financially, I set to work on producing a script that I hoped Greene would find acceptable. I started working with

Shaun McCarthy who had worked with me on *England Made Me*, but we did not really see eye to eye on how to approach the material and amicably decided to end the collaboration on the script.

So I went down to the South of France again and stayed with Jeremy Scott, an old friend from my days with Jim Garrett's various TV commercial production companies. Jeremy, an enchanting public school ex-guards officer, raffish and louche (as he describes himself in the title of a recently published autobiography, *Fast and Louche*), had on impulse opted out of the advertising rat race and bought a converted mill in Provence, part of which he let out as holiday apartments. I rented one of them for a few weeks and started work on the script. Every few days I would take pages down to Graham in Antibes, we would discuss what I had written and I would get his ideas and reaction. I was nervous about taking anything out, particularly the religious concerns of the novel, but to my relief Graham was quite pragmatic about it. "You can take that out" he would say about some theological point. "It will lose you your audience." By the middle of the year (1974) I had a script that Graham said was impressive and read almost like a final one.

Later, when we were trying to cast the picture, I offered the script to Alain Delon's agent for him to consider the role of Eduardo Plarr. I went to Paris hoping to show *England Made Me* to Delon but only his agent turned up.

To my horror, when the credits began to roll, I saw that the title had been changed to *Les Rapacités du Troisieme Reich*, presumably in a vain attempt to attract the cinema-going French by a more sensational title. Nothing came of this attempt to attract Delon anyway.

The search for the leading man went on. Graham and I discussed the idea of Jack Nicholson, and so he wrote me a letter saying that he thought Nicholson perfect for the role, the intention being that I should get it to Nicholson's agent in the belief that a recommendation from the famous novelist himself might arouse the actor's interest or vanity or whatever. It did no such trick. Meanwhile, I had met Trevor Howard, with whom Graham had a friendly relationship after *The Third Man* and who, in our view, was perfect casting for the part of Charlie Fortnum, the honorary consul kidnapped by the urban guerrillas mistaking him for the American diplomat they really wanted. Trevor read the script, loved it and said he would be delighted to do it. I then went to New York to meet Graham's American agent, Monica McCall, and to try and arouse some US financial and distribution interest in the project. Donald Sutherland's agent in London, Dick Blodgett, suggested that Donald might be interested in playing the hero, Eduardo Plarr, who was having an affair with the Honorary Consul's wife Clara. He fixed up for me to meet Donald who was on vacation in his native Canada at the time, so I flew up to Montreal, hired a car and drove to a place called

Malbaie, north of Quebec where Donald and his lovely French Canadian wife, Francine Racette, were spending their summer. Donald is a cool, relaxed and friendly person, and although he had spent some years in England and had even worked on the *Man in a Suitcase* series in an episode directed by Freddie Francis, we had never met before, but we did have one or two mutual friends, like Nic Roeg after whom he named one of his sons. I spent a couple of days chewing over the script with Donald, who seemed somewhat concerned that Eduardo Plarr was not a particularly loving character. Warren Beatty could be like that about women, he observed, but not him. I pointed out that that was in a way the point. Eduardo could not love as Charlie loved his wife, the ex-prostitute Clara who had cuckolded him with Plarr: this was Eduardo's failing and his realization of this led him to his death, whereas old Charlie survived to forgive and forget. There resided the power and humanity of the novel, and this was what I wanted to bring to the screen. Back in New York I arranged with Donald's agents for him to see *England Made Me*, and a few days later got a call from them to say that he would like to play Eduardo, so now I had my two leading actors.

On one of many trips I went to Los Angeles where I stayed with an old friend, the Canadian director Paul Almond. Paul had been at Oxford with me and even acted in one of my student productions. He had directed a series of highly regarded films in Canade starring Geneviève

Bujold and, in one movie, Donald Sutherland. Geneviève and Paul married but subsequently divorced, and Paul was now re-married and living in Malibu with his second wife Joan, a brilliant stills photographer. Like me, Paul was struggling to get various projects afloat. I was sitting in the house one day enjoying a glass of wine and looking out over Malibu Beach when I saw that Paul was standing by the back entrance to his property talking to a familiar face. It was Larry Hagman who lived further along this celebrity strip, and Paul called out to me to come down and say hello to the famous JR of *Dallas* fame. On the following Sunday, we were invited to a lunchtime party at the Hagman's and, as we walked along the beach, Paul casually mentioned to me that Larry did not actually speak to anyone on Sundays. This apparently was some sort of personal discipline related to his need to preserve his voice for his professional commitments on his television show or perhaps a search for some spiritual peace, but it did seem to me that it was likely to make intercourse rather difficult on a social occasion such as the one we were about to take part in. Fortunately, Larry's lovely wife Maj was not similarly bound to silence and was the perfect hostess at a splendid gathering with great food and drink.

The Hagmans' was a top grade Malibu beach colony residence with no expense spared on what was an extremely lush conversion. Between the front and the back of the house was a designer rock pool with great boulders, which had apparently been brought down from Malibu canyon, and an electrically operated glass roof that could be closed when bad weather set in, which was not often. I found myself in a large games room around which was a long shelf loaded with hats of all kinds: English bowlers, French army kepis, Mexican sombreros and Stetsons by the yard. Larry was obviously an avid collector of bizarre headgear. I had already been through some sign language conversation with Larry about the excellent hi-fi system, and we went through a similar *pas-de-deux* over the hat collection. He produced an enormous cowboy hat made of leather that was half white and half black and put it on for my appraisal, but I was not sure how to react, whether he thought it as absurd as I did or the contrary. Without verbal comment from him, which way to respond was difficult to know, so I just smiled in a noncommittal way.

The following year I was visiting Paul again and went for a walk along the beach. On the way back, I saw Larry sitting outside his house with a drink in his hand. I went up to him to say hello and at that moment realized, God help me, it was Sunday again, which meant another conversation in sign language.

I had no luck trying to interest the major American film companies, and, after several weeks, returned to London, somewhat depressed by my failure to stimulate any positive financial interest. I did, however, press on with a second and third rewrite of the script that fell into the hands of

Norma Heyman, a former actress and model who had appeared briefly in one of my Scotland Yard movies, years before she had married the film producer, John Heyman. They both read my script, and they liked it enough to show it to their friend, Richard Burton, who was also impressed and was keen to play the role of Charlie Fortnum. By this time, my free option had lapsed, but I did have a loose working arrangement with Graham's agents that if any interest was shown, they would promote my script as it had been approved by Greene himself. Then I heard that Orson Welles had taken out an option on the book. I rang Graham who confirmed that this was so and that Orson had taken out a month's option, but he did not think that anything much would come of it. Then I heard that Welles' backers, whoever they were, had bought the rights outright, and that seemed to be the end of the affair for me. However, about a year later, *England Made Me* was revived in a West End art house cinema, and I wrote to Graham to tell him about it and to say how grateful I had been for his generosity and patience in the past. He wrote back to me to say that, in the event, Welles had not actually paid up and he had instructed his agents to tell him to either pay up or shut up. I was now able to go back to the Heymans and tell them that the window was open again. They picked up the rights. I did not have the presumption to ask Graham that my script should be included as part of the contract, but hindsight proved that I should perhaps have done just that and risked a turndown from Graham on this point. It was not long before communication with the Heymans became spasmodic and my telephone calls remained unanswered. I found out that, with no reference back to me, my script (that they had not paid a penny for) had been offered to Fred Zinneman, who felt that, at his age, he could not cope with the location problems, and then to Louis Malle, who said rightly that it should be directed by an Englishman. About this time I got a phone call from Graham saying that he thought they were "doing the dirty on me," and he could not have been more right. Heyman decided to get another script written by Christopher Hampton and was finally able to get the film afloat starring Richard Gere and Michael Caine.

Graham never deviated from his support of my attempts to realize one of his best and favorite novels. He did not like Hampton's script and refused to see the film that was made from it, saying in an interview in the *Guardian* that he wanted the film "to be made by a friend of his, Peter Duffell, who had written an excellent script." One of Heyman's excuses for jettisoning my script was that it was "wonderfully written but an extremely literal translation." Perhaps she meant "literate," I don't know, but this is hardly a convincing argument against my version in view of the fact that critics of the film pointed out that—although it remained generally faithful to the novel's dramatic line—it contrived to miss the real moral religious and political drama of *The Honorary Consul*.

Having spent several years pursuing the dream and ending up with ashes in my mouth, it was difficult indeed to be philosophical and just accept that this is the way of the film industry, forget about it and push on to the next challenge.

But I have to confess that—even today—the anger at betrayal and the regret that I did not make the film I felt so deeply about can still affect me.

Inside Berlin

Then another movie happened. A year or two earlier, at a drinks party at the home of my then-agent Dina Lom, the wife of the actor Herbert Lom, I met the American producer, Judd Bernard, who was based in London. Judd was an engaging man with a great sense of humour and an impressive track record of movies, including John Boorman's marvelous *Point Blank.* I ran *England Made Me* for Judd and he liked it enough to offer me a film. I think he appreciated that I had already made this picture set in Nazi Germany, although it was a totally different kind of film from his project. *Inside Out* was a story in the genre known as "the caper movie." A gang of likable villains plans to spring Rudolph Hess from Spandau prison because he knows the secret whereabouts of a cache of Nazi gold. Except that he wasn't called Hess, and the script didn't refer to Spandau. Judd Bernard had made a deal with Warner Bros., who therefore had approval of the casting of the leading characters. Various star names were mentioned, including Lee Marvin, James Coburn and Richard Widmark. In the end we had Telly Savalas, at this time riding high on the *Kojak* television series, plus James Mason, Robert Culp and Aldo Ray. The fifth member of our caper crew was a gentle and highly civilized German actor named Günter Meisner. Günter played an out-of-work actor who, in the course of the story, had to impersonate Adolf Hitler.

I chose the key members of my crew and took them on a recce trip to Berlin. My cinematographer was Johnny Coquillon, whose work I had admired on a couple of pictures he had done for Sam Peckinpah, and my choice of camera operator was Robin Browne, who had worked with me on television series. Robin had a good eye for a shot and was a smooth and sensitive mover of the camera, and I felt he deserved to do a movie. I rang Elaine Schreyeck, who had been my script supervisor—in those days script supervisors were called continuity girls—on *England Made Me* and asked her if she could bear to work with me again. Elaine was the Queen of Continuity at that time, and her credits were quite awe-inspiring. She was affectionately known by the camera crews as "Lady Docker" after the wife of an industrialist, Sir Bernard Docker; said wife made famous in the tabloids for her extravagant lifestyle and expensive clothes. Elaine was always immaculately dressed, sometimes with an expensive fur coat that had prompted the nickname. Above all, she was just ace at her job and both loved and respected by all who worked with her.

Or perhaps, nearly all. When I told her about the picture she expressed some misgivings, saying that she had not been too happy working with James Mason in the past. However, I did manage to persuade her to sign up, which made me happy.

Apart from short sequences set in London and Amsterdam, most of the movie was shot in Berlin. In the '70s, Berlin was still an enclave of West Germany controlled by the Allied powers. There was a French sector, a British sector, an American sector and, beyond the Berlin Wall, the Russian sector. In fact, part of the plot of *Inside Out* was how our heroes could get across into East Berlin where the gold was hidden.

At that time West Berlin was a calculated propaganda demonstration of the values and material wealth of Western democracy. The food department of the big store KVD put Harrods to shame. It was heavily patronized by Soviet officers who came over from the East to do their shopping. The Kaiser Wilhelm Church in the middle of West Berlin stood, without its spire, as a monument to Allied bombing, but the only part of West Berlin that had not been rebuilt after the appalling devastation of the war was the Embassy district, an area of ruined buildings frequented at night by alcoholics and prostitutes. Beneath the blinding glare of large, dazzling neon advertising displays, the city was full of splendid restaurants, posh night clubs and sex shops, along with a vibrant cultural life centering on the Berlin Philharmonic and the West Berlin Opera House. Looking across the wall from the observation platform on Potsdamer Platz, one saw the desolate area with the remains of the bunker where Hitler and Goebbels committed suicide.

East Berlin could be entered through several checkpoints—providing, of course, that one's documents were in order—but the one for foreigners was the famous Checkpoint Charlie, which was to feature in our story. I went through Checkpoint Charlie many times, often to eat at a restaurant called *Ganymede*, much favoured by Len Deighton, and sometimes to visit the opera house—the Komische Oper, which was astonishingly cheap and noted for productions by the famous East German director Walter Felsenstein.

After walking from the checkpoint down the dark and menacing Friedrichstrasse—which, with its empty buildings and no street lighting, felt like something out of *The Third Man*—one finally reached the *Ganymede* restaurant, which sat on a corner. This had two dining rooms, one on the left and another on the right. The proprietors could immediately spot the West Berliners over for a cheap meal and would politely but firmly direct them to the left handroom. The East Berliners were always seated in the room to the right of the entrance, so the twain never did meet. British squaddies also patronized the place and, on one visit, I noticed that a sergeant who was there with a group of men was wearing scarlet. I asked him why, and he said it was a standing order. All NCOs and officers always had to wear full dress uniform should they cross over to the East for any function whatsoever. Allied forces in uniform could move unhindered either way through the checkpoints, but for civilians the time it took to get through Checkpoint Charlie into East Berlin varied a great deal. Sometimes fairly fast and easy, at other times it could take up to forty-five minutes or an hour, depending on the state of mind of the East Berlin border guards who could be bloody-mindedly meticulous in the way they checked your passport. This was probably a reflection of the immediate temperature of the Cold War political thermometer.

On *Inside Out* we spent ten days in Ploetzensee Prison shooting scenes where Telly, James and Robert, dressed as American officers, had managed to con their way inside, assisted by Telly's old mate (played by Aldo Ray), a sergeant in the U.S. unit attached to the guard rota for the famous Nazi prisoner they wanted to spring from jail long enough to learn where the Nazi gold was hidden. At this time Ploetzensee was used for juvenile delinquents who, under the tolerant regime in existence, were allowed home on weekends for good behaviour - not that there was anywhere much they could have gone had they attempted to break parole. But the prison had a much darker history, for it was here that several of the officers involved in the July 20th attempt to assassinate Hitler were brutally tortured and hanged. The execution chamber in a small building in the yard is now open as a museum, but today it is no more than a large, empty room, with little trace of the horrors that took place there. A sort of sterile cleanliness about it reminded me of Dachau concentration camp near Munich, where nothing remains of the prison blocks but their outlines on the ground.

We were given great freedom to shoot where we wanted, and various cells were placed at our disposal. The occupants, moved to other accommodation, had left behind pictures pinned to the walls, family photographs side-by-side with crude pornographic photographs of unbelievable obscenity. Every time we moved from one part of the prison to another, doors always had to be locked behind us, and our ears rang with the incessant clanging and rattling of locks and keys. Whilst we were shooting a sequence of our prisoner, named Holz, walking in the exercise yard, a Scots sergeant turned up with some automatic weapons for the guards, obligingly supplied by the British Army. He looked down on the scene we were shooting and said it reminded him of Hess in Spandau. This, of course, was exactly what it was supposed to do, but we didn't tell him as much. We all heaved a sigh of relief when it was time to get away from the depressing, claustrophobic atmosphere of the place.

Having succeeded in smuggling the Hess character (named Holz in our movie) out of prison, Telly and the others now had to trick him into giving away the location of the gold. The script had them doing this by thrusting him, under the influence of drugs, into a large room in a deserted old government building—which they had decorated with Nazi flags and swastika emblems—where he was faced with the gang now dressed as SS officers. Gunter Meisner, in his role of the out-of-work actor, gave a star performance as Der Führer himself. I felt somewhat uncomfortable with this part of the script and decided that the only way to play it was for the laughs. The actors rose to the occasion, and the sequence caused one critic to talk about the lunatics taking over the asylum.

With Judd Bernard and Telly Savalas
wearing Gunter's Hitler moustache.

When the executives back at Warner Bros. saw the rushes, they sent anxious communiqués to Berlin wondering what the hell the director was up to. This was, after all, supposed to be an action movie, not a comedy, and in their book such scenes did not happen in this kind of picture. The plot twist was that Holz tells them where the gold is hidden, which turns out to be in an underground bunker in East Berlin. This means the gang has to go through Checkpoint Charlie still pretending to be American officers. But it was impossible to film anywhere near the Berlin wall: if we did, the Russians would switch on flood lights and loud music to prevent our working. The only thing we could do was build our own replica of the checkpoint in a West Berlin side street. In the middle of our night shoot, a somewhat inebriated East Berliner on his way home produced his papers for our scrutiny. He thought he had arrived at the real checkpoint and was somewhat bemused by the laughter at his expense.

When we were filming the sequence of the gang dynamiting their way into the bunker, an elderly passer-by told us he had a bust of Hitler—would it be of any use to us? We said it certainly would and gave it pride of place on a dust-covered desk in the underground room. We were too polite to ask why he had held on to this souvenir of the past, but we appreciated his offering to lend it to us.

In the next plot twist our heroes had to get the befuddled and doped-up Holz back into prison before the

American guards were relieved by the Russians, but they found the way across a bridge blocked by a broken-down lorry loaded with planks of timber and—as a sweating and nervous Sergeant Aldo Ray sits in his office looking at his watch——with no possibility of removing it in time for Telly and the others to make the deadline. Then Telly has an idea. They bribe the lorry drivers to build them a ramp over the lorry, and Robert Culp drives their car up and over the obstruction.

This, of course, called for a stunt driving team. Judd had contracted Remy Julienne, who was responsible for the incredible sequence with the Minis in *The Italian Job*. Remy and his team came up from Paris to do the shot, along with one or two other stunt sequences, and were fascinating to watch. We sat around waiting with three cameras ready to roll, set up in key positions that Remy designated because he knew exactly where the car would land. It was a morning's work for one important shot that would last but a few seconds on the screen—and no possibility of a second take existed. Remy set it all up with incredible care and patience and finally gave me the okay he was happy to go. When the car landed, exactly where he said it would, sparks flew spectacularly as the chassis hit the ground. He managed to keep the car going long enough for the shot to cut nicely to our heroes laughing with glee as they continued on their way to the prison. The car was a write-off, as he had prophesied, because the suspension left much to be desired, but we had a duplicate standby to use for the rest of the filming.

The film was fun to shoot and worked well. I enjoyed working with the entire cast and crew, except for one. I have had a happy relationship with most actors, but I am sad to say that James Mason and I did not hit it off at all well. Matters were not helped when we were shooting early one morning in the reception of the Schweizerhof Hotel, where we were living. It was a simple scene where Telly walked up to the reception desk to ask for the character, Major Ferben, played by James Mason. James, as always the complete professional, was standing by on set

James Mason and Robert Culp in West Berlin.

long before I needed him. Telly, however, hadn't arrived. I set up the scene with his stand-in, and then went off to the hotel restaurant for a coffee while my cinematographer Johnny Coquillon lit the set. A worried Elaine came to tell me that during my absence James had said loudly to various members of my crew that the director should not set up a shot without the artists being present. Here was I, a relatively unknown film director, in confrontation with a famous actor who, for all I knew, could have cost me my job. I called my assistant director over and said I was going to my room and would be grateful if Mr. Mason and the producer, Mr. Bernard, would join me there to sort this out. In minutes I had an agitated Judd on the phone asking me what had happened and I told him. He asked me not to stop shooting but to please go back on the floor, and he would sort it out with James. It seemed to me that the only action I could take was to have it out quietly with James myself, which is exactly what I did. I explained to him that I had a tough schedule and, much as I would prefer always to have the actors present, I could not hold up shooting. In any event, this was a simple scene, requiring no more from Telly than moving from out of camera up to the reception desk, so it was perfectly reasonable for me to set it up before the actor arrived. James backed down, saying he was only joking, but this unnecessary little encounter only added to our already somewhat uneasy relationship. It saddened me, as I had always respected James Mason as an actor. I had a little bit of a problem with Robert Culp, too. I don't think he was happy playing second string to Telly Savalas. He had had a successful television series of his own and had also recently directed a picture himself. I had a sneaky feeling he thought he should have been directing this one. On the other hand, Aldo was always a pleasure to work with and had a wonderful knack on the set of being able to smooth over any little differences involving his fellow stars. His personal life was at this time, I think, somewhat chaotic and unhappy, and he was living in a caravan somewhere on the edge of Beverley Hills. The insurance medical report on him was not good, but Judd was prepared to take a chance. We were, however, slightly concerned when he arrived at our hotel having consumed a vast amount of free alcohol on the flight over from the States. A short drying out period was indicated, and Judd assigned the duty of keeping a discreet eye on Aldo to one of the supporting actors, but, after that, Aldo's behavior and performance were immaculate, and he was a joy to have on the set. I remember him telling me a marvelous story about his relationship with Humphrey Bogart on the film, *We're No Angels*, about a group of convicts on Devil's Island. Aldo had been a professional boxer and at that time was new to the film business. If anything went wrong on the set, he told me, Bogey would point the finger of blame at him. Aldo got so fed up with this ploy that he finally threatened to land one on Bogey.

Bogart laughed and suggested they have a drink together after the end of the day's shooting, which they did and were good friends ever after.

With Telly, I got on well. If I made a suggestion or request, he would say, "You got it," and that was it. I think the only problem I ever had with Telly was when he arrived back late from a weekend visit to London where he was promoting his album on the television show *Top Of The Pops* and, until he finally turned up on the set, I had to shoot close-ups of the other actors in the scene, pretending he was there.

We were once driving to our location past the Kaiser Wilhelm Church when some young men standing nearby recognized Telly and shouted out to him. Telly waved back, calling "Love, baby, love," then asked me in his inimitable Noo Yawk accent, "Who are dose guys?" "Turkish guest workers," I said. "Berlin is full of them." All Telly's Greek patriotism came out. "Fucking Toiks!" he said. "Why didn't ya tell me?" What could I say?

Is the true story of what happened in Germany too terrible for it to be treated as a subject for a comedy action thriller? It may be that comedy is the only way we can live with it. Mel Brook's *Springtime for Hitler* is perhaps the most brilliant and outrageous comedy treatment of the Nazi horror after Chaplin's *The Great Dictator*, but Chaplin made angry fun of Hitler before the full horror of what the Nazis did was revealed to the world.

As a result of his performance as the out-of-work actor who has to impersonate Hitler, poor Gunter frequently found himself playing Der Führer on British television. Gunter and I became good friends and often met on his visits to London, sometimes outside the Tate Gallery of which he had fond memories. During the war he had been a POW, working on a farm in England, somewhere in the West Country. On one occasion the people he was working for had lent him a suit to replace his uniform so that he could go to London to visit the Tate.

Several years later I was in Berlin again on a location recce for another project, with my friend the writer, John Howlett, and a fellow director named Ken Grieve. I felt a sentimental journey to the Ganymede restaurant was a good idea, and so we presented ourselves at Checkpoint Charlie where the East German security officer asked us to show our wallets for inspection. This was a common request usually made to check out how much West German currency we had with us, but Ken rather unwisely had his television company pass with him, which aroused some curiosity. After a pleasant meal in the Ganymede, a most bizarre meeting took place, which in retrospect we decided must have been because of the contents of Ken's wallet. The frontier guard must have reported it. As we left the restaurant, we were accosted by a nondescript-looking man in a shabby blue overcoat, with the collar turned up, carrying a violin case under his arm. He appeared to be studying the opera and theatre advertisements on one of those round iron display units that one finds in Europe, and he greeted us in English. He commented on the fact that we had visited Ganymede but said that a more interesting cafe, patronized at one time by Berthold Brecht, was only a short distance away and that we should certainly visit it. Being rather curious, we agreed, and as we entered this crowded, smoky room full of local men, an uncomfortable silence seemed to descend on the place. We ordered drinks at the bar and a table mysteriously became free. We all sat down with the drinks we had paid for with the small amount of East German marks allowed at the frontier in exchange for West Germany money. Because the chap was carrying a violin case, we had assumed that he was probably a musician from the Opera House Orchestra, but he made neither mention of what he did for a living nor any reference to music whatsoever. He told us that some years before he had been to Sri Lanka, which he called by its old name of Ceylon, but had nothing further to say about that part of his life or any other, although he did talk much about West Berlin and alleged friends and contacts he had there. As we talked, it became clear that he was really trying to find out if we had any ulterior motive for being in East Berlin. He referred to a West Berlin friend who was a journalist and then talked in a round about way about Jehovah's Witnesses, whom we were aware were known to cross over and get into trouble with the authorities for their attempts to convert the locals to their beliefs. He tried one or two other similar ploys to get us to commit ourselves to some expression of criticism of the Eastern bloc, but without success. When a glance at a clock showed us it was time to make our way back to Checkpoint Charlie, he suggested we had plenty of time because we did not have to go through before midnight. We knew better and said good-bye. Had we taken him at his word, it would more than likely have meant a night in a police cell and some kind of police interrogation. We were pretty sure that our encounter with this rather seedy fellow was no accident. His presence must have been the result of a telephone call from the zealous frontier guard to some counterespionage unit.

At the historic moment of November 9, 1989, when the Berlin Wall came down and East Berliners were able to flock into the consumer paradise of West Berlin, I rang Gunter at his home. He told me that it was impossible to get a banana anywhere in the city. The East Berliners had bought them all.

Flight

In 1978 one of the big productions at Pinewood Studios was the first *Superman* movie, directed by Richard Donner and starring the then-unknown young actor Christopher Reeve. I had a call from my agent, Duncan Heath, to tell me that he had heard from their production office offering me a job as a second unit director. Feeling somewhat insulted by the suggestion that I did second unit work for other directors, I suggested to Duncan that he tell them to take a running jump. Duncan came back to tell me what sort of money they were offering. It was considerable, and because I was in need of some highly expensive dental work at that time, I could not refuse the offer.

So I went down to Pinewood to meet the producer, Pierre Spengler, and director Donner, and I was soon given my own office and camera crew headed up by cinematographer Alex Thomson. The old Hollywood director, Andre de Toth, was also doing second unit work, so I figured he was, like me, a bit financially pressed at the time. Andre was doing complicated back projection work on the back lot, and I was allocated one of the large stages. Money and time seemed of little concern on this production, and whenever I offered to Dick various alternatives for a shot or sequence, he would always tell me to shoot it all ways and we could chose the best in the editing rooms. I had to do lots of flying shots with Christopher. He conscientiously insisted on doing them himself even though some of them could have been completed by a stunt man as the flying harness was not the most comfortable experience. As he was needed by the first unit most of the time, it meant that after lighting the set, which consisted of a blue sky backing around the edge of the stage, we had to sit about doing nothing for hours on end waiting for Christopher to be available to us. The camera crew and studio hands would pass the time playing card games or reading the sports papers. I would retire to my office and do some script writing for my own projects.

In one sequence I had to fly Superman and his girlfriend, Lois Lane, around the moon. Instead of moving them once I had got them up into "the blue empyrean," which would have been fiendishly difficult, I had the bright idea of moving the moon itself—a cut out—across the backing behind them. This worked well and Stuart Baird the editor and I cut the sequence together to show to Dick. For a music backing track I found a section of Richard Strauss' *Thus Spake Zarathustra* that fitted the sequence rather well. When I ran the sequence, Christopher, who came with Dick to look at it, said he thought it was fine but "the music was shit." I had to point out, rather acidly I fear, that it was actually inspired by Nietzche's Superman concept and that I suspected that when John Williams came to write the score, he would probably be inspired by Richard Strauss anyway, which, of course, he clearly was.

I worked for twelve weeks on this monster production and decided that I really did not want a credit on the movie. Neither Andre nor I had one, but I note we are both there on the Internet Movie Database anyway.

I was having lunch one day at Pinewood Studios with the film composer, Bernard Herrmann, famous for many film scores and particularly those for Alfred Hitchcock and Ray Harryhausen, when he told me this wry and bitter joke: A film producer and a composer were lost in the middle of a vast desert. They had been walking for days and were dying of thirst. Suddenly they saw in front of them a beautiful, great silver dish full to the brim with ice cold water. They stared at it in disbelief fearing that it was no more than a mirage. The composer reached out a trembling hand and touched it. It was real. He turned to the producer and said, "If we carry this with us and carefully ration our drinking, we might make it back to civilization." The producer replied, "Okay, but tell you what— let's piss in it first." A director telling it would probably replace the composer character with one of his own calling, but in any case the joke defines the uneasy relationship that often exists between the money and the creative talent.

Fortunately, this is not always so. One of the nicest producers I ever worked with was Joe Janni. Joe was a Milanese who had lived in England for many years, and his position in the history of English film making over two or three decades is awe-inspiring. A very cultured man and a wonderful producer for writers and directors to work with, he was never dictatorial and believed that ultimately a film was the work of its director. If he felt that some artistic compromise had to be made to satisfy the men in suits, then he would say, "Put it in the script but when it comes to it, you shoot the film the way you feel it should be done." It was Joe who gave my old Oxford friend, John Schlesinger, his first chance in feature films with *A Kind of Loving* after recognizing his talent from his work in documentaries. After that, together they made five more films including *Billy Liar*, which brought fame to Julie Christie, *and Far from the Madding Crowd,* which starred Alan Bates, Peter Finch and Christie. Joe liked my work on *England Made Me* and offered me a film based on a *novella* by Francis King. It was a story of Helen, a somewhat feckless divorced mother of an eleven-year-old daughter of whom the father had legal custody. She absconds to Greece with her daughter whom she virtually kidnaps, planning a happy-ever-after life for the two of them with her lover, a journalist who works in Athens. When they arrive, they find that he has left for another assignment elsewhere, and Helen has to face the painful truth that he has deserted them. Her angry ex-husband sends a private investigator in search of them. He finds that she has begun an affair with a Japanese man working in Athens who has given them a home in his apartment. The Japanese, who is resented by the daughter, turns out to be a terrorist. When Helen decides that the only real future for her little girl is back home in England, the Japanese puts them on a plane with a bomb inside a doll that he has given to the child. They are saved from death only because the child, hating both the present and the giver, leaves it on an airport bus that explodes on the tarmac.

Joe had a script which he was not particularly happy with, so I was in for a major rewrite. He had hoped that Julie Christie would accept the major role, but, when Joe returned from a visit to Hollywood to discuss the project with her, he told me that she did not want to do the film after all. Joe, who had helped make her into a star, I think felt somewhat let down, and I was disappointed. Anyway we carried on with many script conferences broken up by civilized lunches with good wine while Joe and I explored casting possibilities. One of the leading characters in the story was a Mrs. Setty, a rather lonely, elderly lady in somewhat reduced circumstances who lives in the same hotel as our heroine and her daughter when they first arrive. She strikes up an affectionate relationship with the lonely little girl that survives their departure when Helen takes them to live with the Japanese. We rewrote the part several times to tailor it to fit several different stars who might be attracted to the project. The names of Katharine Hepburn and Ingrid Bergman came up among others, but I cannot now remember what subtle changes we might have made in the script to suit them. At one point I was on holiday on the Greek island of Alonyssos and doing just that, sitting under a shady tree and banging away on a portable typewriter. The next major challenge was to change the setting from Greece to Rome, as Joe saw the possibility of Italian money as part of the financial structure of the movie, and this meant an Italian actor to play the terrorist instead of the Japanese in Francis King's original story. So the Greek *evzone* doll that the Japanese gives to the little girl had to become a Vatican Guard, and I did a location recce to Rome to meet production designers, costume people and others arranged for me by Joe's Rome associate, Luciano Perugia. We were also now assembling an excellent cast. Katharine Ross and Franco Nero accepted the leading roles, Olivia de Havilland the part of the old lady and Trevor Howard was set to play the private investigator, whom I had turned into a somewhat Graham Greene-ish character.

Then disaster struck. Joe's old friend Nat Cohen, who was the power behind the English distribution company Anglo-Amalgamated (the company that financed the Scotland Yard series and the Edgar Wallace B-features that started my career), decided to retire, and the running of the company was taken over by two men, Barry Spik-ings and Michael Deeley. As always seems to happen in such cases, the board was swept clean of all projects that they had not initiated, which meant our picture was one of them. So my script gathered dust on a shelf, and sadly I never made a movie with Joe Janni.

Joe's associate producer on our project, Luciano Pe-ruugia, also had a property which he asked me to direct and co-script. I spent months working on the script with trips to Rome to discuss it with Luciano and meet various creative people who might work on the project. Then Lu-ciano found a business man in Canada who was prepared to finance the picture if we could get Steve Guttenberg and Kim Catrall as our stars, so he and I went to Holly-wood to offer the script to Guttenberg who was having a great success with the *Police Academy* movies. But he was not interested in working in Europe so another proj-ect bit *the* dust. It was not a good year.

Journey by Rail via White City

My first assignment in live television was a short dramatic piece written by the talented South African novelist, Justin Cartwright. Shot entirely in the BBC White City studios using up to five video cameras, it was my first experience of shooting a studio television play.

These studio dramas were rehearsed in a large building in west London, known as the Acton Hilton, with the set plan simply marked out on the floor. By the end of the rehearsal time, the director would have to produce a shooting script with each shot, which might be static or tracking, and indicate which camera would pick up the shot. Because the camera cables could get tangled during shooting, standard practice was for the director to work out a plan using movable pieces of cardboard representing the cameras, each one on the end of a piece of string (representing a camera cable) pinned to the studio wall at the terminal points. On the day of shooting at White City Studios, after a run-through on the set that would probably be the first time the actor had seen—let alone worked on—the actual set, the play would then be recorded from beginning to end, stopping only for correction of mistakes or meal breaks. During the shooting, the director would have to sit with the technicians in the control room overlooking the studio floor. A major source of irritation would be that he could communicate with his actors only via the assistant director on the set who would be picking up any instructions on his headphones. During actual shooting, the production assistant sitting beside the director would literally call the shots by intoning the number of the camera that should record the action at each moment of the drama. The mixer would then switch that camera to the recording decks, so in effect editing was instant. All five cameras would probably be running continuously, and the monitors in the racks above the control panels would show what each camera was picking up. But what was actually recorded would be only the shot on the camera marked in the shooting script. The director had to remember this and realize that, even though the camera operator on one of the other cameras might be offering up a striking shot, it would not be there to be cut into the picture at the end of the day because it had simply not been recorded. Therefore, barring the odd mishap and subsequent patching in a video editing suite, at the end of shooting the play would exist as a completed piece with perhaps only titles remaining to be shot and the adding of sound effects and music.

The story was about a white South African of English

origin who had been sleeping with his African housemaid, which was a criminal offence in the days of apartheid. The dramatic centre of the story was the confrontation between the man concerned and a Boer police officer who harbored a personal resentment because of something that had happened earlier between their two families. Michael Cochrane played the main character, and as the Boer policeman I cast John Castle who was so good as the future King John in the Peter O'Toole, Katharine Hepburn film, *The Lion in Winter*. The two actors served Justin and myself wonderfully, and we got pleasing reviews in the national dailies.

There were other studio-based productions for the BBC. *Murder Rap,* a script by the playwright Michael Hastings about racial prejudice, was a mix of studio work on video and some film. *Bright Eyes*, by Peter Prince, was one of a series of dramas set in the near future called *Plays for Tomorrow*.

Historically television was, and to some extent remains, a writer-oriented medium. In the beginning, when "live" television drama was shot on studio stages using multiple video camera techniques, television drama was largely based on existing theatrical plays, and the text was religiously observed and changed only if the writer agreed to it. This accounts for the fact that even long after major drama pieces were based on original scripts and shot mainly, if not totally, on film, the BBC still called them the *Play of the Week* or whatever. When I won a British Academy of Film and Television Arts award for my film of Stephen Poliakoff's script *Caught on a Train*, it was still categorized as being the "Best Single Play."

Who makes a film—the writer or the director? Some writers fondly believe that the function of the director is simply to point the camera at the actors saying their immortal lines. Gore Vidal certainly thought that the director was the one member of the film unit whose services could actually be dispensed with. But as the great director Nicholas Ray once said, "If it is all in the script why make a film?" to which could be added "in which case, the obvious thing is to go write a novel."

The producer David Puttnam, for whom I made a fairly successful picture, also expressed reservations about the value of a director but from a different angle:

> "*I find directors to be less honest than producers,*" he is quoted as saying in a book called *Calman at the Movies. "I think they frequently hide behind high intent when often what you are dealing with is low purpose. The job description is so damaging. I feel sorry for directors, in a way, because the ethos and the culture of a film director, what a film director is, is so out of whack with what the job really is.*

I'm sure a lot of them have a tremendous
problem not wearing jodhpurs. They are
acting out a role."

So there go Alan Parker, Hugh Hudson, Roland Joffe and a few others, including myself. After reading that, you might be excused for thinking that the following quote came from one of those Jodhpur obsessives, but actually, it is from a letter from David himself to the actor Spalding Gray, quoted in his book *Swimming to Cambodia*:

"Dear Spalding,

On Sunday, we all start to make a very
difficult and worthwhile film … as ambitious
as I have ever attempted … which will, by
the time we get through it, have thoroughly
tested us all …By nature, by sheer scope
and theme, The Killing Fields *is one of*
those few movies by which all our careers
will undoubtedly be judged…

Roland and I found a speech of President
Kennedy's this week in which he said
'I realize that pursuit of peace is not as
dramatic as the pursuit of war. Frequently,
the words of a pursuer fall on deaf ears. We
have no more urgent task'… These words,
spoken twenty years ago, have never

been more relevant. We have a unique opportunity with this film to make our contribution …

In the years to come, it is my honest belief that The Killing Fields *will be the very first to be mentioned explaining and justifying the way we spent the best and most difficult years of our lives."*

That certainly rates high on the Richter Scale of Intent, but "low purpose"? Perhaps his last sentence will do:

"If we pull that off, then every form of possible reward will undoubtedly follow and we will deserve it."

For some cinema films of well-known theatrical pieces, of course, the director does simply point the camera with various degrees of efficiency at the performances in front of it, but they are recognized as such and not considered as pure cinema, whatever that might be. Film, as the cliché says, is a visual medium at its best. Audiences remember a John Ford movie, for example, for the power of its imagery and not the dialogue, however important that may be in storytelling terms or character definition. But the creation of mood, atmosphere and dramatic tension is in the hands of the director who is the ultimate film maker, whether he aspires to wear jodhpurs or not.

One important area of writing for film is in the adaptation of works in other disciplines, mostly the adaptation of novels. Again some novelists think that adapting for the screen is or should be no more than putting numbers against each scene in their book, but the structure of a movie and its narrative rhythm are quite different problems. Often the story and dialogue need to be simplified. A long speech that is effective in a novel or in the theatre can be leaden and dull on the screen, and it may be necessary to reduce the number of characters in the story. When the assignment of writing a screenplay is given to another writer, that writer may consciously or not change the mood and meaning of the story in a way that mirrors his own preoccupations rather than those of the original creator. In extreme cases, the result can be that little is left of the original work except the title, which accounts for the cynicism and anger many novelists and dramatists feel toward the film industry. But although changes may be necessary for a number of artistic and economic reasons, the ultimate aim of the adapter should be to remain true to the meaning of the original work in spirit, if not in the letter.

Having now made a moderately successful offering for the BBC, I was offered a film based on Margaret Drabble's novel, *The Waterfall*, and once again I found the existing script did not, by any means, honor the book. So with the permission of the producer, Colin Tucker, I embarked on a major rewrite going back to Drabble's original. *The Water-fall* was the story of a young Oxbridge-educated woman who rebels against her comfortable upper middle class background and marries a young musician from a family her parents consider below them. The marriage is not a happy one, and she has a passionate love affair with the husband of her closest friend, her cousin Lucy. The novel was stylistically original and also an early feminist state-ment. It was not easy to adapt, and Drabble herself said that she would have found it difficult to do. I had to find a cinematic way of realizing the two distinct voices that Drabble used in the novel—one the voice of the romantic Jane, laden with passion and guilt, and the other the sane, coolly self-analytical woman who, as the first-person nar-rator of the story, steps back from time to time and tells the reader how it really is. My solution was to cut from the romantic scenes to a composed Jane speaking directly to camera, her first line being: "It won't do, of course, as an account of what took place."

For the role of Jane I was lucky to get Lisa Harrow, whom I had seen on stage with the Royal Shakespeare Company, and for her cousin Lucy, Caroline Mortimer. We cast Robin Ellis, the handsome hero of the popular television series *Poldark*, as James, Lucy's husband and Jane's adulterous lover. We had worked together before at the BBC on the Peter Prince story *Bright Eyes* (which I mentioned earlier). A young actor, Stephen Boxer, played Jane's sad husband who earned his living as a musician. Stephen was, in fact, an accomplished performer on the lute and guitar, and we had one scene in the Queen Elizabeth Hall where he sang a piece by the Elizabethan composer, John Dowland. BBC budgets being what they were, we could not afford enough extras to fill the concert hall, so I had to resort to shooting through a door at the side of the stage with every available member of the crew occupying the relatively few seats in the auditorium that were visible.

I can have nothing but praise for my actors who served me and Margaret Drabble to perfection. I was particularly happy with a scene where the two cousins meet after the car accident that almost takes James' life, and Lucy's anger at her cousin softens into forgiveness and understanding as the two women sit on a bed together getting slightly tipsy.

The reviews were excellent. Sean Day-Lewis in the *Daily Telegraph* called it "a lovely aching work of art." *Broadcast* said it was "a most satisfying and impressive piece of television, in every respect a most distinguished piece of work," and I was flattered when Margaret Drabble herself said in an interview that she had nothing but praise for my adaptation, which she described as both inventive and faithful to the original.

Then the producer, Kenith Trodd, who was noted for his work with Dennis Potter, offered me a script written by Stephen Poliakoff. Trodd and Potter had been at Oxford together and had a close relationship—albeit in its later years a somewhat tempestuous one. Trodd was a writer-orientated producer and Potter was a writer who wanted directors to do exactly what he had written. The idea of changing or removing a line of text was absolutely out of order. The result was, of course, some of the best television drama in the height of the single play era—the time when, as I have already said, the different nature of film was not yet totally understood within the confines of the television drama departments. Trodd was a Machiavellian figure in television drama who totally understood how to manipulate the system to advantage at the BBC Television Centre. He had been responsible for a great deal of the best output from its drama department at that time, and not only work by Potter.

He had a sort of Heathcliffian unruly appearance, lived, it seemed, largely at the Centre in his office which was festooned with his shirts and jeans, and was notorious for his jackdaw habits and for never missing a freebie handout whatever form it might take. On one occasion, he had notoriously broken through a union picket line to pick up a free buffet at some industry function, and whenever on location always could be seen collecting up the little jam pots and bread rolls left over at breakfast by the unit. Apparently, when crossing to America for a showing of a production there, he even walked the length of the airplane to collect any such items left by passengers at the end of their in-flight meals and would always, as it was jokingly noted by the crews, turn up for the lunch break on location. Although these oddities of behavior were gently mocked by the technicians, people who worked on his productions held him in great respect because they knew that for Ken the end product was what really mattered.

My own relationship with Kenith was somewhat checkered, possibly because, as he once pointed out in the middle of a heated argument over some artistic issue, we came from two different traditions—but in the end we made one of the most remembered pieces of television drama of the time. *Caught on a Train* was a story about a train journey across Europe that turned out to be a nightmare for a young go-getting British publishing executive on his way to a book fair in Salzburg. His torturer was an elderly Viennese lady who endlessly made impossible demands on his goodwill but who in the end gained his affection and respect. The train movie is an old and much-loved cinema genre, and Alfred Hitchcock's *The Lady Vanishes* is, of course, a classic. Stephen oddly denied that his script was in any way influenced by the master, but as far as I was concerned Hitchcock was certainly influencing me, and several critics picked up on the connection.

The piece was fascinating, full of the sort of brilliant oddness and *aperçus* of Poliakoff's writing as well as some maddeningly unconvincing twists of plot. The practical problems were fairly daunting, as it was originally con-

ceived to be partly shot in the studio. How one was supposed to achieve that when it was mostly set on a moving train journey that started in Ostend and then moved
across and through various German cities was beyond me,
for it was clearly a totally filmic piece, which was what it
finally became. Ken Trodd realized this at some early point
of the pre-production period and adroitly maneuvered a
situation where we managed to shoot the piece as it should
be done. We cast the brilliant Michael Kitchen as the pub-
lisher and entered into a transatlantic dialogue with Lotte
Lenya, who was an exciting possibility for the old Viennese
aristocrat. However, she decided that she could not physi-
cally face the location problems at the time of year that
we were shooting and gracefully bowed out. We then approached Dame Peggy Ashcroft who had, as it turned out,
been Stephen's original idea for the role. Peggy accepted
the part, which made all of us very happy indeed. With all
the supporting roles cast, the really big problem of how
to shoot the film was now our prime concern. For me, it
was a jigsaw puzzle of how to put the train together from a
most complicated series of parts. Some of the film would
be shot in Europe and some of it in England. We found a
privately owned tourist attraction near Peterborough, the
Nene Valley Railway, which specialized in continental rolling stock. We planned to shoot a number of sequences
there, but they did not have a sleeping wagon, which our
story needed. Good work by the production department

unearthed a *schlafwagen* in Belgium, which was no longer in use and which the Belgian railway company was prepared to pass to the English owners of the Nene Valley project. The BBC made a deal with them which meant that they always had facilities to shoot on the railway in exchange for buying and delivering the wagon, and so it was brought over from Belgium.

A long sequence was set in Frankfurt where the maddening Frau Meissner makes our hero leave the train in search of a meal, during which they end up in the Opera House buffet and nearly miss the train continuing on its journey. It was therefore practical to shoot part of the story on a real German train, particularly the incident where Michael Kitchen is taken off the train at night by German policemen who suspect him of being some sort of terrorist and subject him to all sorts of humiliations. The German railway company not only was extremely cooperative but also provided us with a splendid dining car for the unit meal on a night shoot. For the scene in the Frankfurt Opera House, I chose the sounds of the Richard Strauss opera *Der Rosenkavalier* coming from the auditorium. I love the opera and felt it would be dramatically perfect to use it, with its resonances of old Vienna. I said to Stephen that I wanted a line here for Peggy who, hearing the beginning of the famous last trio decides she must go into the auditorium to listen to it, saying "I remember Lotte Lehman" who was, of course, a great opera star and one of the most famous Marshallin of all time.

Peggy and Michael worked wonderfully together. She never complained although a tough schedule and a great deal of night work put considerable strain on her. She had had an operation on her knee not long before filming began, and she had to do lots of walking about in the cold streets of Frankfurt in the middle of the night. She studied the Viennese accent with the help of recordings of Lotte Lehmann, among others, and I was later assured, by people who knew, that her accent was impeccable. Michael's role was not an easy one. He had to be a foil to Peggy's demands of him, getting newspapers for her at the start

Peggy Ashcroft and Michael Kitchen in the Frankfurt Opera House.

of the journey from Ostend and nearly missing the train as a result, having to suffer embarrassment when she makes a scene in the train dining car, and generally being put upon by the elderly Viennese monster—in other words, to react rather than be a prime mover of events. Michael was superb in the role and wonderfully unselfish. The result was that he came over forcefully and commanded sympathy and not contempt, which might have been possible with a lesser actor even though his character was, in fact, a pushy and not particularly admirable person. In recent years, of course, he achieved a great success in the internationally popular television series *Foyle's War*.

The budget did not allow night shooting when we

Peggy and Michael on Frankfurt Station.

returned to England, and set to work on the Nene Valley Railway, but we still had to shoot night sequences on the train, which presented me with yet another problem. The branch line was only two or three miles in length, but a little way down the line from the station and goods yard I saw a tunnel that solved the problem for me. So every day we took the carriages down into the dark tunnel. John Else, the cinematographer, then had his electricians swing lights to flash through the carriage windows so that it looked as though we were on the move. The camera was also always hand-held with a slight movement to simulate the rocking of the train. On a location recce in Germany, we had taken a camera with us and shot bits and pieces from a real moving train to inter-cut with our actors' scenes. I had drawn sketches of the layout of the train, showing where the dining car, the sleeping car and other passenger coaches were in relation to each other, and in this way I could assemble all the pieces of my jigsaw puzzle to form a coherent whole.

I had long admired the work of the jazz composer Mike Westbrook. His music is remarkable for the way he has brought into the jazz scene a whole range of European cultural references to poetry, theatre and visual arts. I felt that Mike would be the ideal composer for our film and he took on the assignment, producing an outstanding music track mirroring the dramatic tensions of the piece.

Caught on a Train was nominated for various awards

that year. I had no idea that we had won before the BAFTA dinner, but I had a pretty good idea that we might have when I found Ken had joined our table and not the ITV one, where he could have been as he had produced for the commercial station a series of Dennis Potter plays that were also in the running. It was perhaps typical of dated television thinking that this essentially filmic piece should be categorized for a Best Single Play Award. For direction I took away the BAFTA doorstop, but in addition Peggy got the best actress award presented to her by her old friend, Alec Guinness, as well as getting the same award at the Monte Carlo television festival. We also gained the National Press Award and several technical category awards, making a total of seven, which was a quarter of the BBC's prizes for that year. Not bad for one drama entry that some twenty years later was still considered in a *Radio Times* poll as being one of the best programmes ever shown on television.

About the same time, the film was issued on a DVD in a series of Stephen Poliakoff's work. The cover read, "Stephen Poliakoff's *Caught on a Train*," and as a result various internet retailers gave him the director credit. This was a minor irritation for me, but nothing like finding that on the DVD commentary provided by Poliakoff and Trodd (which normally takes place between the director and actors), the latter went out of his way to damn my work with faint praise, pointing out in a disparaging way that

I had been brought up in a classical movie tradition and seemed to have planned every shot, suggesting that the film might have been better if I hadn't!

When Peggy died a few years later, the film was re-shown on BBC as a memorial to her. I received a letter from the great director Fred Zinnemann. Fred wrote:

> *"On this sad occasion of Peggy Ashcroft's death it was a lovely consolation to see* Caught on a Train *last night. I thought I should tell you what a wonderful piece of work it is in all departments. Sad as we all were, we truly enjoyed seeing it and noticing that it had not aged one bit."*

For me this was something of which I was more proud than the BAFTA accolade.

Experience on the Isle of Man

Shortly after getting that nice note from Fred, I visited him one morning for coffee. He talked about his time in Hollywood and told me a wonderful, funny anecdote about Billy Wilder, one of his oldest friends who had, like Fred, left Berlin when the Nazis came to power. It was a story that Wilder told against himself. It seems that a young autograph hunter accosted him on numerous occasions brandishing his pen and autograph book. This happened enough times for Wilder to recognize him, and finally he asked the young man why he kept asking him to sign his book when he had done so several times already. The boy answered that if he could get twelve Billy Wilders, he could swap them for one Steven Spielberg. I think Wilder may have invented the story, but it was a wryly humorous reflection on the nature of fame in the movie business.

David Puttnam, now Lord Puttnam, was the producer of the Oscar winning *Chariots of Fire*, among other distinguished and commercially successful British films. David had seen some of my work and offered me a film in a series he was producing for television called *First Love*. This was about a young girl student who takes a vacation job in a Welsh holiday hotel. The film was called *Experience Preferred But Not Essential*—a title suggested by me—and was one of the first Channel Four films to be aired after the station opened. It was set in the 1960s, a sort of "rites of passage" story, for our heroine Annie, a shy young girl lacking in self esteem, comes through the experience a wiser and more confident young person. Wales presented a problem because we could not find a location that looked right. However, our location manager found the seaside resort of Douglas on the Isle of Man, the small island off the northwest coast of Britain, famous for the TT motorcycle races. Douglas seemed to be set in a time warp and looked perfect for the movie. Just on the edge of the town, up a road overlooking the sea shore, we found a hotel which worked perfectly. On the west side of the island, the little town of Peel also had attractive location possibilities.

We had a cast of relatively unknown young actors. For the waitresses in the hotel we found a group of girls working together in an Islington pub theatre, and the team work they had developed there paid off wonderfully. Our heroine Annia, played by a young actress named Elizabeth Edmonds, wearily carries her suitcase up the road from the bus stop and reports for duty to Helen, the manageress. Then she is led by a complaining porter up into the squalid maids' quarters of the hotel where she meets the other waitresses: Mavis the tough realist (Sue Wallace), Paula (Karen Meagher), Doreen (Geraldine Griffith) and Arlene (Maggie Wilkinson). Annie is plunged straight into the hectic live of hotel workers. I had noticed how the real hotel guests waited impatiently for the dining room to open for the evening meal and I shot a sequence showing Annie's first experience of the organized chaos of the event: the guests outside the locked doors; the waiters and waitresses in position waiting for the owner to give the signal to open up precisely on the hour; then the Gadarene rush as the hungry guests pour in to find their tables. It was sadly removed from the final cut however, but not with my approval.

The workers in the hotel were a real bunch of odd balls, losers and eccentrics and their personal and sexual lives were complicated to say the least. The head waiter Ivan had the disturbing habit of sleep-walking at night into the waitresses' bedrooms. The other waiter, Hywel— a slick young man prone to combing his hair in the hotel restaurant and dipping his comb into the nearest water jug—was sleeping with Paula, which caused great embarrassment to Doreen, with whom she had to share a room and even the bed. Arlene, the oldest of the waitresses, found herself, to her great consternation, to be pregnant. The manageress Helen (Arwen Holm), who was far from popular with the other female members of the staff, was having an affair with the hotel owner, and Mavis and Doreen were also having problems with their love life.

Douglas contained a marvelous variety theatre that we felt we ought to use, and June Roberts, the screenwriter, quickly dreamt up a sequence in which Hywel entered a tacky talent contest. The result was one of the funniest sequences in the movie and Alun Lewis, who could play the guitar, gave a splendidly hilarious performance doing an impersonation of Elvis Presley. Later, when the girls and their various boyfriends gather in the hotel bar, Doreen and Paula do their own rendition of Helen Shapiro's 1960s hit *Walking Back to Happiness*. Annie finally finds her own happiness with Mike, the head chef, a cheerful young Scot, played by Ron Bain. She is also taken under the wing of the sophisticated Helen. When the summer job is over she walks back to the bus stop with a new self-

The waitresses in *Experience Preferred* - Karen Meagher, Geraldine Griffiths, Maggie Wilkinson,Sue Wallace and Elizabeth Edmonds.

confidence, her suitcase carried for her by an admiring young fellow traveler.

Never shown theatrically in England, the film was picked up by Sam Goldwyn Jr.'s distribution company in America and ran successfully in movie houses all over the States. Reviews were very good and we even got an excellent one from the dreaded Vincent Canby, who had viciously slaughtered *England Made Me*. The movie ran for six months in one New York cinema alone, resulting in an article in *The Guardian* from their New York correspondent who wrote that it had become a dinner table conversation-piece in the Big Apple. At the time I would not have thought that this essentially parochial little film would ever have traveled further than Lands' End.

This success in America both puzzled and pleased me. I think its popularity may have been because its central theme of a young person's experience of working her way through college somehow struck a chord. American billing also advertised that it was "a film from the producer of *Chariots of Fire*," so that certainly helped a bit as well.

I had a few "points" as they are called in the business, which means a small share in the net profits of the picture. Points are something you don't normally see because, by the time creative accounting has taken place, a film is usually shown not to have gone into profit—unless it has been such a smash hit that the accountants can't hide it. Long after the film was made, I was delighted to receive

In good company at the Westland Cinema, Los Angeles.

a quite healthy check from David as part of my share in the profits, and this was only because he had engaged in a long and tiresome legal battle with the English distributors of the film which forced them to reveal the true accounts.

An Indian Love Lyric

"I wasn't born, I jus growed." This quote, attributed to Topsy in *Uncle Tom's Cabin,* could have been just as easily uttered by the television mini-series.

I don't know who dreamt up the term, some American network genius I imagine, but one can have an idea of how it came about. A fat, best-selling novel sells millions of paperback copies, many of which end up on the shelves of charity shops. It is read by commuters on suburban trains and city metros; it fills the shelves of airport newsstands and is consumed by jet-lagged middle management executives and hordes of reddening bodies on Mediterranean beaches, its pages smudged by suntan oils. Then, as the movie industry no longer makes films from this kind of blockbuster novel, it comes to the notice of some network executive who sees its potential as TV material. It is too long for a single TV movie and too short for a series format, but at the same time likely to attract the interest of star actors no longer a pulling force in cinema films but still a good marquee attraction for the small screen. So what to do? The answer is simple: make it as a two- or three-part programme. So what to call it? Well, a series it ain't, and a TV Movie of the Week it ain't, either, so how about—got it—a mini-series!

Sometime around the beginning of 1982, my agent, Duncan Heath, his ear as always close to the ground, heard of the impending production of a mini-series based on a 900-page novel about the British Raj in India in the latter part of the nineteenth century. It was called *The Far Pavilions*, and it was written by M.M.Kaye who, with her husband, a professional soldier, had spent many years in the Indian subcontinent. *The Far Pavilions* told the story of Ashley Pelham-Martin, a young Englishman whose family had died during the Indian Mutiny and who was brought up as a native by his nurse who had saved him from a similar fate. He becomes a servant in the household of an Indian royal family and is befriended by a little girl princess. When, during the Indian Mutiny, British soldiers finally find him, he is sent back to England to be educated and, as a young man, becomes an officer in the famous Corps of Guides who served on the North West Frontier. He is torn between his loyalties to England and his deep love and understanding of the people of India with whom he had lived as a little boy. Then seconded to escort a wedding procession across the great expanses of India, he discovers that one of the two young brides is his childhood sweetheart Anjuli. They fall in love, but Ash has to see her married to the repulsive ruler of Bithor. After a series of adventures involving battles in Afghanistan, the famous siege of the British Residency in Kabul in 1789 and other dramatic action pieces, all ends happily for the two, and they ride off into the sunset towards the Himalayan mountains, which have always symbolized a land of mystery and beauty for them.

Oddly enough, I had a short time before been offered an assignment as co-director on a TV version of Paul Scott's trilogy of novels about the Raj called *The Jewel in the Crown*, but I clearly would not be running the show and instead be answerable to Christopher Morahan, who was both producing the series and directing at least half of the episodes. I decided after a great deal of agonizing and great reluctance to turn it down. I felt that if it was a success, Christopher would obviously get most of the credit. If it failed I would get a share of the blame.

It seemed worth putting my name forward for this Indian project. Geoffrey Reeve was producing. I had known him for some years as an advertising agency TV commercials producer before he branched out into the feature world. Geoffrey was a portly, expansive character, partial to cigars and St. James' shirt-makers. He always exuded an air of a man skilled in expense account diplomacy, wheeler-dealing and fund raising, activities he was impressively good at. He had even directed two films based on best-selling novels by Alistair MacLean, the rights of which he had managed to acquire at a time when a Maclean novel was a hot film property. Neither film was exactly a critical or box-office success, and one of them had been largely re-shot by a highly skilled film professional Don Sharp, who, for contractual reasons, got only a second unit director credit. The script for *The Far Pavilions* was written by Julian Bond, a writer with a number of excellent television credits whom I had known for even longer than I had Geoff Reeve, for we were undergraduates together at Oxford. There had been a long-standing but quite friendly feud between us, because I had written a cutting and would-be witty review for the undergraduate magazine, *Isis*, of a college production of the Jacobean drama, *'Tis Pity She's A Whore*, in which Julian had played Vasques, the villain of the piece, giving a performance that I had singled out for my most poisonous shafts of critical venom. Despite never having totally forgiven me for this scurrilous notice, Julian had, with great generosity of spirit, suggested to Geoffrey Reeve that I was the man for the job.

So here I was in this trendy watering-hole. As it turned out, the lunch was not with both Geoffrey and Julian but with Julian alone, as Reeve was lunching at another table with a "money man." But he came over to greet me and apologize for not joining us. Over a bottle of excellent claret, writer and prospective director discussed the problems of translating the book into film. I mentioned other projects that might be about to materialize. Julian expressed the hope that I would see my way clear to do *Pavilions*, and, having eaten and drunk rather well, we went our separate ways, leaving Geoffrey to sign the bill.

Our next meeting took place in Geoffrey's offices in a suite that was actually leased, or had been, by Carl Foreman. The walls were still adorned with awards, photographs and other memorabilia of his cinematic successes like *The Guns of Navarone*. Superimposed on these were Geoffrey's own holy relics, lots of photographs of himself with horses at race meetings, winning cups and drinking champagne with top management personalities of the leading tobacco companies for whom he made cinema and TV commercials. Also hung there was a photograph of himself with President Zia of Pakistan, both grinning in friendly fashion at the camera. More interesting, though, was the promotional material for the project in hand: costume designs and photographs of Indian Palaces, elephants and the snow-capped peaks of the Himalayas, as well as pictures of actresses who might play Anjuli, the half-caste Indian-Russian princess who is the heroine of the novel.

I also met the author, Molly Kaye, and her husband, Goff Hamilton, during this time, two utterly charming people who seemed to typify the history of the British Raj.

By the end of February I had a nice letter from Geoffrey saying, "Welcome aboard," and an invitation to his country estate for an early informal production get-together. He owned a most pleasant large house and extensive land out-side Aylesbury. As we talked around the problems of what was going to be an ambitious production indeed, one could watch, from the drawing room window, the village cricket team playing on their field, which was actually on his land. It was the first of a number of meetings at the producer's manse, and I had the feeling that it put us all in our place as hired hands. At this meeting, at which were present Nick Gillot, Geoffrey's associate producer, and the costume de-signer, Raymond Hughes, I got the first intimation of front office control, which in its small way was imitating the be-havior of the all-powerful American majors. As he filled up the champagne glasses, Geoffrey threw out casually that the role of Ashton Pelham-Martin, the hero of the story, was going to be played by Roger Rees, a leading actor with the Royal Shakespeare Company. The idea that the director might at least be consulted about casting major roles didn't seem to enter into it. Roger Rees, an actor for whom I had great respect and admiration, was playing Nicholas Nick-leby in a splendid RSC dramatization of Charles Dickens' vast novel (long novels always seem to be described as vast), but for me Rees was essentially a theatre actor. The film camera has never been particularly kind to him, and I thought it a bit odd to cast a man in his middle thirties to play this swashbuckling and macho young rebel Ash, who is supposed to be about eighteen when he returns to India as a young subaltern in the Guides, the elite regiment on the North West Frontier. What we needed was a romantic hero in the Heathcliffe mould, a young Olivier, Errol Flynn, Douglas Fairbanks and Robert Taylor all rolled into one, and with the best will in the world, Roger Rees was not that. I wondered what the hell Reeve and the English company Goldcrest, which was then riding high, were thinking about. Although the films would be produced by Reeve's own production company, they would be financed by Goldcrest in association with the American cable and TV company, Home Box Office, and therefore, quite clearly, these two companies would in their various ways have quite a say in how the show was handled. But I held my peace for the moment. Shortly after that I was at the Richmond Theatre with an old friend, the actor Constantin de Goguel who had worked with me on *Inside Out* and several other films, and in the crush bar during the interval we saw Roger Rees talking to another fine actor, Robert Lang, who had come to a sticky end in my horror movie, *The House That Dripped Blood*. Observing him surreptitiously, I found my earlier misgivings quite justified.

At this point the series consisted of eight episodes of one hour each. It was only later that it was reduced to six one-hour programmes which would, in major territories, be shown as three two-hour episodes, conforming to the true mini-series format.

Meanwhile back at the ranch, my agent Duncan Heath was making a deal, but nothing was signed. Time went by without a firm commitment, and I had no idea if the project was going to become a reality. It is normal practice in the film industry to hire a director at the earliest possible moment so that he can begin working with the writer and get himself prepared for the actual event, which in this case would mean location reconnaissance trips to India and a crash course in Indian culture and religions as well as the history of the British Raj. But this was not to be with *The Far Pavilions*. Unlike film producers like Joe Janni, Geoffrey Reeve did not seem to be prepared to risk a little capital on hiring a director, with a get-out clause if the film did not get off the ground, even though he had already spent a considerable amount going on location reconnaissance trips without one.

Several expensive visits had already been made to the Indian subcontinent by the producer, the associate producer and the writer, some locations pinpointed (in the event I actually used none of them), and contacts made with local film production people and others. While these trips may have been pleasurable for all concerned and were certainly valuable to the writer, they weren't of much value to the man who was finally going to have to lay himself on the line and get the story on celluloid.

As it happened, some changes were going to be made in the whole command structure before Goldcrest and HBO gave the go-ahead, which was not forthcoming by the middle of the year. So, when Duncan rang up to say that David Puttnam's production company Enigma would like me to make a modest little low budget movie in their Channel Four series called *First Love*, I had to say yes, even though I would have liked to spend the time reading up about India. I have already written about *Experience Preferred*, and when I returned from the Isle of Man to begin editing it, I found that my agent was beginning to get dusty answers from Geoffrey Reeve about the contract. At first we did not know why. Other directors' names were being bruited around, but what had I done to blot my copybook? I sat in Duncan's office while he had a telephone conversation with Geoffrey. Duncan said something like, "Let me get this right, Geoff. You are saying that Goldcrest don't want Peter because they are unhappy with his work on *Experience Preferred*?" The answer, which I could not hear, was clearly in the affirmative. Duncan put the phone down and we looked at each other. What he did then was agenting at its best. He rang David Puttnam who had already expressed to me his ignorance of why Goldcrest were pussy-footing about director approval, and gave him the gist of his telephone conversation with Reeve. David was furious about the allegation that seemed to be a criticism of him as producer. Up to that time, nobody at Goldcrest had seen a foot of the material that I had shot in the Isle of Man, and David personally was happy with it. The film had come in on budget and schedule and, taking it as a personal slight, he even went so far as to threaten legal action against Geoffrey Reeve.

At the same time, Duncan contacted Jane Deknatel, then Head of Production at HBO, who was in London at that moment. Jane said they certainly had director approval, to which Duncan said, "Fine, so would you care to look at the work of my client who is supposed to be doing the picture for you?" Jane sat in a Wardour Street theatre the next morning looking at *England Made Me*, said okay and that was it. The crisis was over. Geoffrey said that perhaps he should have looked at *England Made Me* himself—an astonishing admission that he had not already done so, seeing that it was this film that had influenced his writer, Julian Bond, in his recommending me for the job in the first place. From this I inferred that he had not made any strong defense of his choice to Goldcrest when the issue arose. Anyway, thanks to David's support and Jane Deknatel's approval of my work, I was now well and truly "aboard."

But why Goldcrest should have turned against me still remains to this day something of a mystery. Could it have been because I had shot a few scenes for *Experience Preferred* early in the schedule that were not in the script, although they are in the finished film, so that I looked like one of those "difficult" directors whom you don't need on projects like *The Far Pavilions*? Possibly. Or could it be that Goldcrest's production man, Terence Clegg, had taken exception to me on this score, even though at that time I had never met him or anybody else at Goldcrest for that matter? David hinted at something like this when, after the dust had died down, he remarked to me that perhaps it was time that people in our industry were judged by their work and not idle gossip. The irony was that I nearly lost my livelihood for the next two years because of a small film which, in the event, turned out to be the most successful one of the *First Love* series. This is how a director's reputation and livelihood can be put in danger by minor production executives anxious to save their own backsides in case of argument.

But if my head didn't roll, other heads did. When Goldcrest agreed to back the film, they insisted on nominating production people across the board. Nick Gillot, who had worked on the project with Geoff Reeve for a long time, was elbowed out, and a production executive named John Peverall took over as executive producer, a title whose meaning has changed considerably over the years but which in this case meant "line producer," that is to say the man who would actually control the production. John had had long and varied experience including tough location jobs like *The Deer Hunter*. I had said that I would like, as production designer, Tony Woollard, who had worked with me on *England Made Me*. Tony is a man of great visual flair and imagination, and he had spent lots of time in India working on what turned out to be an abortive project based on the best-selling novel *Tai-*

pan. Goldcrest, however, nominated Bob Laing who had worked as art director/second-in-command to the production designer on Richard Attenborough's film *Gandhi*. So Tony was out very early on. The costume designer, Raymond Hughes, was already at work before I arrived on the scene, and the composer had also been chosen by Geoffrey Reeve. This was, in fact, my old friend John Scott who had composed the score for my Graham Greene film, so I was quite happy about that. But my nomination for editor Tariq Anwar, who had won a BAFTA award for his excellent work on my film *Caught on a Train*, was also not approved by Goldcrest. The point about all this is that areas which are normally the director's prerogative, that is to say the creative team with which he is going to work, were being chosen without any consultation with him whatsoever. Whereas this did not please me one bit, I have to say that in actual fact, the people concerned were among the best that the profession has to offer, and the support that they gave me turned out to be quite fantastic. That one or two old friends might have felt that I had let them down was something that I had to bear, for nobody else was going to shed a tear.

Offices were now set up in Lee Studios at Wembley and we got into the problems of casting, scheduling and budget. Every day messages came through from on high that another 500 or 750 thousand dollars had to be carved out of the budget. This was already quite tight considering the ambitious nature of the script, which contained great scenes of military action, set pieces of great splendor like the wedding of the princesses to the dissolute Rana of Bithor, an enormous procession that wanders its way across the Rajasthan desert for a large part of the action, fights up the Khyber Pass and the burning of the princesses in the funeral of the Rana—the "suttee" scene—all of these "with a cast of thousands." The next creative appointment that had to be made was that of cinematographer. John Peverall told me that Jack Cardiff, one of the most distinguished cameramen, was available. I had lunch with Jack, whom I had not met before, liked him instantly and said to John that I would be most happy if Cardiff would accept. We couldn't do better. Jack, who had won an Oscar for the Powell and Pressburger movie *The Black Narcissus*, had photographed so many wonderful pictures and worked with so many of the great actors and actresses of the movies: Katharine Hepburn and Humphrey Bogart in *The African Queen*, Ava Gardner and Bogart again in *The Barefoot Contessa*, David Niven and Raymond Massey in *A Matter of Life and Death*. Jack had also directed around twelve movies, including a highly praised version of D.H.Lawrence's *Sons and Lovers*. At this point we had yet another nomination from on high, and I felt at this point I had to stick my heels in and say I wanted Cardiff, and that was that.

Next thing I had to meet Sir Richard Attenborough who

was Chairman of Goldcrest and, as the maker of *Gandhi*, the Indian hand. I attended a trade showing of *Gandhi* in the Rank Theatre in Hill Street, one of a series of such showings at which Dickie was going to be present and at which he expected to have the pleasure of saying hello to me. As usual on these occasions, the reception rooms attached to the theatre were laid out with canapés and bits and pieces to nibble. We retired thereto and, being mighty hungry by this time—*Gandhi* being a fairly long film and not having had any dinner—I began to lay into the sausages on sticks. Dickie had arrived just before the end of the movie and was circulating to receive the congratulations that were his due. I kept an eye open for a propitious moment to introduce myself. When that moment came, I moved towards the famous actor, film maker and chairman. "Good evening," I said. "My name is Peter Duffell..." Before I could get any further, up swept a media lady. "Oh Dickie," she gushed. "I'm dying for you to meet ..." whoever it was and, grabbing Dickie's arm, dragged him in the direction of whoever the lucky person was. I retreated back to the sausages on sticks and had another swig at the *vin ordinaire*. When the audience with whomever was over and Dickie once again seemed approachable, I returned to the fray. "My name is Peter Duffell ..." I said once more and had hardly got that out when another media lady (or was it the same one? They all looked alike to me) sashayed up. "Dickie darling, do come and meet ..." And off Dickie went again. My wife sensibly had stayed with the canapés. I moved back beside her and muttered, "I'm fucking well going home, I've had enough of this Mahomet and the mountain shit." At which point I turned to see that Dickie was again free and we were more or less looking at each other. I advanced and said my ritual piece again. Dickie looked a little blank, I think in the confusion of the moment, for I am sure he was as embarrassed as I was angry, so I hastened on to make things clear. "I'm about to direct *The Far Pavilions*." To my intense relief, Dickie's brow lightened, and he grasped my hand warmly. He courteously acknowledged my wife, and we sat down together in some nearby chairs. An Indian lady in a sari came up and said a few words to Attenborough, then glided away. "Have you got a costume designer?" asked Dickie. "That was so and so who worked on *Gandhi*. You ought to use her." I pointed out that I already had one who, in fact, had been appointed before me and said that as a fellow director, he would understand that I didn't take too kindly to all these appointments, which were normally the director's prerogative. I thought that was pretty good as I knew perfectly well that some of them had been nominated by Dickie himself, but he accepted the thrust with good grace and then went on to talk about Goldcrest's production executive, Terence Clegg. "He's a good man, Terry," he said. "A bit of a rough diamond, but he knows the business and his judgment is sound. If he tells you somebody or something's no good, you know it's accurate." As I had good reason to believe that in Terence Clegg's opinion I was in the category of the no good, I found this judgment questionable to say the least. But I held my peace.

As the picture on the wall of his office bore out, Reeve had contacts in Pakistan through his tobacco advertising activities and we were going to explore the possibilities of shooting the part of the film that took place on the frontier in Pakistan itself. The problems might be enormous because of the strained relations between India and Pakistan, which would make traveling between the two countries with loads of film equipment an operational nightmare. None of the professionals thought the idea was really on, but we had to go there to see for ourselves. In any case it was invaluable for the creative people to see the actual places where the story took place, even if we couldn't shoot in them.

So a party consisting of myself, John Peverall, Kevin O'Driscoll the accountant, a production manager named David Anderson who had worked on *England Made Me* as assistant director, Bob Laing the production designer, and Molly Kaye's husband Goff Hamilton flew to Rawalpindi in Pakistan on our first real location recce. Goff was with us because he knew Pakistan well and had many contacts with members of the government and the military who might be of use to us. Goff, of course, had served in the famous Guides Regiment himself. One of his ancestors,

Wally Hamilton, had died fighting bravely in the assault on the British Residency in Kabul during the second Afghan War in 1879 and is featured in the novel as Ash's friend. Goff was, not surprisingly, *persona grata* with important people there, and his presence was extremely valuable in smoothing our way through possible bureaucratic difficulties. We duly checked in to our hotel in Rawalpindi. Goff had brought with him from England a full dress Guides uniform that he intended to give to the Guides museum, and he had arranged to present it to General Iqbal who was Minister of Defence at that time. Goff asked me if I would like to join him. Knowing the Pakistan and Indian passion for cricket, I had taken my Marylebone Cricket Club tie with me, and this seemed an appropriate occasion to wear it. As we waited at the hotel for a taxi to take us to the General's house, Goff mildly remarked that it was remarkably like the Guides regimental tie. I thought no more of it at that moment. We waited for the General in a palatial living room in his house regaled with rather nasty, sweet-tasting soft drinks, alcohol being forbidden in this Muslim country. When the great man, wearing a spotless white jellabah, finally swept in, after warm greetings between the two old soldiers I was introduced to him. His eyes went straight to my tie. "Were you in the Guides?" he asked, somewhat icily, I felt, as he must have thought that I could not possibly have been even a ranker in such a distinguished regiment, and anybody less like a Guides officer than myself I could not imagine. A moment's embarrassment and then inspiration: "No sir," I replied. "It's actually a Marylebone Cricket Club tie. I thought I might wear it in honor of Pakistan's victory at Lord's last week." "Ah," said Iqbal, somewhat mollified. "I see." I had, in fact, been present at the slaughter in question where Imran Khan's men had given us such a pasting. I am not sure whether or not he thought I was taking the mickey, but the meeting passed pleasantly enough, although he cast the odd covert glance at my neckwear, and when we shook hands on leaving, his eyes remained firmly riveted to it.

The rest of the week seemed to consist of dreary visits to officers' messes where relics of the British occupation, portraits of British officers, silver ashtrays, cups and other memorabilia, lists of regimental honors and polo trophies, et al, were side by side with narrative paintings of the more recent wars between Pakistan and India. The officers all spoke a sort of dated upper class English slang, and the maps of the sub-continent ominously showed no frontier between Pakistan and Kashmir, over which India and Pakistan have fought several times. Having just read *Freedom at Midnight* I knew why, but I couldn't resist innocently asking the C.O. of the Regiment why this was so. I remember his answer as being somewhat evasive.

From Rawalpindi we moved on to Peshawar by road, from where we were going up the Kyber Pass to the border of Afghanistan. We went right through the Pass with a small but necessary armed escort of the Frontier Force. We had firm instructions that if we stopped anywhere we should not move off the road. It seemed the government had little real power in the area. Either side of the road was tribal territory, effectively ruled over by the Pathans themselves. It soon became clear that even if we did film in Pakistan, we would not be able to shoot in the Khyber Pass itself. We were the ones who would get shot, not our picture. At the border with Afghanistan, Goff had to inspect a guard of honor laid on for him at the frontier post. The guards all turned out in their best turbans with a sort of colored starched fan stuck in the side. This was the time of the Russian invasion of Afghanistan, but local people seemed to have freedom of movement to and fro across the frontier, and no sign of the Russian presence was evident, although I was told that road signs of the Checkpoint Charlie variety had now been taken down. Although a valuable experience for me in terms of the feel of the picture, by this time we realized that Pakistan did not present a viable proposition for filming. No local film industry existed to speak of, and all sorts of bureaucratic problems seemed possible.

We visited Mardan, where a fort had been the Guides regimental headquarters for over a hundred years. I walked round the military cemetery with Goff. He pointed out two of his friends' graves and said quietly that he might himself have been there. Even in his time the pattern of conflict on the frontier had not changed since the beginning of the British presence there. The tribes would refuse to pay taxes, the British would send out a punitive force, men would die and British soldiers' bodies would lie on the hillsides obscenely mutilated. Kipling wrote a line inscribed on a stone monument at the starting point of the road up the Khyber Pass:

> *"Two thousand pounds of education*
> *killed by a ten-rupee jezail"*

We also made a trip up the Swat Valley, now, tragically, a centre of conflict with the Taliban, where we passed the night in a government dak bungalow. We ate tough, old chicken for supper (I think we had heard it protesting its demise an hour or so before dinner). A Tannoy loudspeaker of some vintage erected on a tree just outside our bedroom windows, woke us up at some barbarous hour with loud recorded sounds, highly distorted, of a mullah calling the faithful to prayer. From Pakistan, after a brief visit to Kashmir, we flew on to Delhi, India, and were met at the airport by Moyna Singh, a contact who worked for the British India Tobacco Company from whom Reeve had tried unsuccessfully to get finance. We booked in at the Welcome Group Hotel. For the next few weeks, I flew in and out of Delhi without seeing the city, for from there we went more or less straight on to Jaipur, the capital city of Rajasthan, where we planned to shoot most of the picture anyway.

Jaipur proved to be the answer to many of our prayers. We had not only the magnificent City Palace for the great wedding scene in Part Two, but also the Amber Palace for the imaginary City of Karidkote and parts of the palace of the Rana of Bithor. I did a lightning tour of the wonderful palaces of the Pink City, as Jaipur is called because of the predominance of a special kind of light red in the architecture. Jai Singh, one time Rajah of Jaipur, had the city laid out on the model of a classic European city. On a hill just outside the city was the Amber Palace—I could take an elephant up the hill to get to it. Then after ascending a great flight of steps, I entered a splendid courtyard with graceful colonnades and a kind of ceremonial majesty. It was breathtaking and just the location for the Court of the Rana of Bithor where Ash Pelham-Martin and Kaka-Ji with their attendant lords would be received on the arrival of the wedding procession.

Our biggest stroke of luck was finding a small palace at a place called Samod, about an hour's drive from the city, which we could use for the Residency at Kabul. Samod also worked well for other parts of the story. What was particularly good about it was that it sat under the walls of a fort, just as the real building sat under the walls of the Bala Hissar, the great fortress of Kabul, and from which streamed the attackers who massacred the tiny British Force of Guides in 1879. And going round to the other side of the fort on the hill, we had a perfect location for the final encampment of the Wedding Procession outside Bithor. The only problem there was access. "No problem," said Bob calmly. "We'll make a road up to the plateau." And that was exactly what happened after negotiations were satisfactorily concluded with the head man of the village. We actually provided useful employment and income for local people, so we were welcome. Many other possible locations in and around the city would have to be checked out, but clearly Jaipur would be our main base for the filming. What remained were the military cantonments that featured in the narrative and that we expected to find in Delhi, various odd temples and palaces and some long shots of Bithor that we found in Jodphur. Rajasthan is a magical part of India. As you drive out of Jaipur, fields of wheat and shrubland give way to marshlands and the vast rocky Rajastan desert, which was where we would shoot the scenes of the wedding procession in which the heroine Anjuli and her sister are taken from their home state to be married to the villainous Rana of Bithor. Camels were everywhere, beasts of burden for the people of the region, and all around us were the astonishing fortresses built on every conceivable vantage point in the landscape, their long thick walls undulating across the hillsides. Nothing was more beautiful than when driving out into the countryside, in the middle of a great expanse of sandy-coloured terrain, one suddenly came across women working in the fields, their saris in brilliant greens and red and yellows providing a dramatic splash of colour. We traveled around in old Ambassador cars, the standard vehicle in India—no air-conditioning, which was not funny in August and September—and ended up each day hot, tired and filthy. As I stood under the shower at the end of each day, pounds of Rajastani dust and dirt washed out of my hair onto the floor of the shower.

Julian Bond joined us there and came with us for the rest of the trip. Geoff Reeve, who was also planning to join us, was taken sick in Bombay with kidney trouble and had to return home to London for a nasty operation. In the pink city we moved into the Welcome Group Hotel, the Mansingh.

Bob Laing, the production designer, who was an old India hand, whispered to me that the real place to be was the Rambagh, one time palace of the Maharajah of Jaipur and now *the* hotel in the city, certainly the place to stay when we started filming. Bob is a rotund, cheerful man with a military moustache, who looks surprisingly like the popular image of an Indian Army colonel, a fact that we often pulled his leg about. But under this equable exterior was a man of infinite resources, painstaking attention to detail and a vast knowledge of and feeling for the subject in hand.

He gathered around him in his art department and in the construction department a team of people who were among the best in the business. Orson Welles said that the cinema was the greatest electric train set a boy could have to play with. Bob and his team gave me the best train set that was possible in the circumstances and made sure that it worked from day one of the shoot. (More of that later).

We paid a visit to Bombay, the centre of the Indian film industry universally known as Bollywood, to meet the Indian casting director who would be looking for actors for us for many of the parts. We also met the jolly, roguish Saeed Jaffrey who was in line for the role of Bijou Ram, the villainous courtier who had tormented the young Ash as well as set up various political skullduggeries. I found him in his hotel room relaxing on the bed surrounded by dishes of Indian food, copies of *Playboy*, film magazines and books on Ingmar Bergman and Luis Buñuel. Saeed was commuting between London and Bombay, where he was working in a number of different films at the same time, which is customary in Bollywood. I also met the lovely actress Jennifer Kendal, wife of Shashi Kapoor, who had starred with her sister Felicity in *Shakespeare Wallah*, and I was delighted when Jennifer accepted an important role in my film.

We returned to Delhi by road through Agra. This meant, of course, a visit to the Taj Mahal. Before leaving London, I had been told that the way to see this wonder of the world was by the light of the full moon, so I had insisted that we should arrive in Agra before dusk on September 3. The team had managed to humour me without upsetting the schedule unduly, and we did arrive in Agra late in the afternoon of the 3rd. By the time we had checked in at the hotel and cleaned up, the sun had set and the moon was out. Julian and I made our way to the Taj, both of us fearful that the photographs in a million Indian restaurants would cheapen the moment. We paid for our tickets and I kept my eyes downcast as we walked through into the conventional long shot position. Then I did a slow pan up. The effect was tremendous. It was true. This was the way to see this wonderful vision for the first time. Those black and white photographs, sometimes occupied by members of the Royal family, had done nothing to spoil the moment. The Taj seems to float and shimmer, and the steady stream of visitors is reduced to an awed silence. The fabric is covered in semi-precious stones that catch the light of the moon in its journey across the heavens, and so the beautiful symmetry seems to be alive and trembling. I was glad I had listened to the advice that at the time I thought to be just a bit of romantic nonsense.

The unit continued on its way back to Delhi, leaving Julian and I to come on twenty-four hours later. This was the sage suggestion of Bob, who sensed that we needed time together to sort out some of the script problems. This we managed to do while paying another visit or two to the Taj to see it at dawn and at sunset. One of the problems of the "vast sprawling" novel was the complexity of the dynastic struggles in the Kingdom of Karidkote, home of the Princess Anjuli. The wives, uncles, aunts, brothers and sisters involved in the plots and conspiracies were many and confusing and added to them were courtiers, counselors and faithful old servants, goodies and baddies in bewildering numbers, many of them with identical characteristics. I suggested getting rid of many of them and reducing the intrigues to the most understandable dimensions possible, so that on the one side we had one naughty little spoilt rajah and his evil henchman Bijou Ram, and on the other a younger princeling and sister Shusila, along with kindly old uncle Kaka-Ji and the despised half-caste, half sister Anjuli, the heroine of the novel. Julian agreed with some relief and said it needed an irreverent and fresh approach to the script to sort out this kind of problem.

Then it was back to London and once again to the casting sessions—numerous because we had such a very large cast. The leading roles were a nightmare to fill. The American backers, Home Box Office, had casting approval for at least the main parts. They submitted four names of American actresses as acceptable. Three of them wisely turned it down as they clearly saw how unsuitable they were for the role. This left the field clear for the fourth—Amy Irving, at this time in her mid to late twenties, with blue eyes not seen in any Indian princess in any period. After a not very fruitful search among possible bankable names known to the Americans, we ended up with Ben Cross, who played the Jewish athlete in *Chariots of Fire*, as our hero, Ashton Pelham Martin. Omar Sharif accepted the role of the Pathan horsemaster, Koda Dad, who was the hero's spiritual father in his early years, and Robert Hardy took the part of the commanding officer of the Guides Regiment, both perfect casting. Rupert Everett was cast in the role of George Garforth, the Anglo-Indian half-caste. I was thrilled when Sir John Gielgud accepted the role of Sir Louis Cavagnari, who led the tiny British force in Kabul, all of whom, including Wally Hamilton V.C., died heroically in the siege of the British Embassy by Afghan Army mutineers. Various promising young actors came to talk to me about the role of Wally Hamilton, including Kenneth Branagh who clearly had his own agenda for the future, which did not really include a supporting role in our epic. It was finally taken by Benedict Taylor, a handsome young actor with all the qualities of a Boys' Own Paper hero. He fought and died heroically and also acted with great charm and personality.

I met Sir John Gielgud for the first time over lunch at a splendid restaurant in Jermyn Street—the Ecu de France. It seemed that he had talked about me with Peggy Ashcroft. Apparently I had passed the test, and Peggy had said, he remarked, that I often argued with the producer, which was true but which he implied did not meet with his disapproval. He also expressed some concern about the fact that the script required him to ride a horse in certain scenes. The last time he had had to ride, he said, was some years before in Tony Richardson's film, *The Charge of the Light Brigade*, and he hadn't been too happy about that, either. I did my best to reassure him, muttering about stunt doubles, but when it came to it, in a scene where the British entered the Residency in Kabul, he did ride—with dialogue while on horseback to boot.

An actor friend of mine, Barrie Ingham, who had played Claudio in the production of *Much Ado about Nothing* that John had taken to New York, told me a wonderfully funny story about it that has now gone into theatre mythology. Many of the small parts were played by New York actors. John, who was directing the production as well as acting in it, was rehearsing the wedding scene, which is a dramatic high point of the play. He told one of the bit part actors that he wanted him to walk centre stage, kneel before the altar, cross himself and move to stage right. The actor in question slouched on, performed a perfunctory "Hi God" sort of gesture before the altar and moved across stage. "No no!" said John. "I want you to behave like a great English lord." The actor, obviously a product of the Actors Studio, walked down to the footlights, peered at Sir John sitting in the stalls and said, "But, Sir Gielgud, like who am I? Where have I come from?" "You silly boy," said Sir John, "you've just come from off stage."

I had dined out on this story on several occasions and could not resist asking John if it were true. He smiled gently and said, "I really can't remember, but I do hope so."

I had taken to India with me a newly acquired Arden edition of *Hamlet* thinking how nice it would be if John would sign it for me. After all, I had actually seen him

in my youth playing the Dane the last time that he performed the role in England at the Haymarket theatre. He
obliged and the inscription reads, "*To Peter in memory of
our Indian love lyric from an ex-Hamlet.*" If any future bi-
ographer of our great actor should come across my copy
of the play, I trust that it will not be wrongly interpreted.

Some roles still remained to be cast when we flew to
Jaipur for the last weeks of pre-production preparation.
Before I left, I had a meeting with Jake Eberts, the affable
head of Goldcrest. Jake impressed on me, as if I didn't
know, that we were working to a tight budget and schedule: the story of my life. He said it was not like a feature
picture, and if I didn't get a scene in the can on schedule
it wouldn't be in the film. This seemed to mean that there
would be a hole in the narrative, but I merely nodded un-
derstandingly, for I had been this way so many times before. By the time I returned, the Art Department under
Bob and the Costume Department under Raymond were
hard at work. The sumptuous look of the picture owes everything to them and to the great Jack Cardiff. I felt it a
supreme honour to work with Jack, who was always cool,
calm and collected, who worked fast and gave me confidence in what I was doing as well. My great good fortune
was to have him with me.

I was sitting having breakfast on the terrace of the
Rambagh Hotel in Jaipur when some alarming news was
first broken to me. I saw John Peverall and his assistant,

David Anderson, walking towards me across the lawn and something told me that all was not well.

"Are you sitting comfortably?" John asked me. Then he told me that the Italian actor, Rossano Brazzi, was being proposed to play the major role of Kaka-Ji, the elder states-man of the Kingdom of Gulkote and uncle and advisor to the young princesses. I could not believe my ears, and I composed an angry, and far from politic, fax to Dickie At-tenborough, questioning the sanity of whoever had made this ridiculous decision. Why, you might well ask, have an Italian actor in the first place? The reason was the old film industry reason for doing something absurd: money. Some sort of Italian deal in place which meant a guaranteed small return from that country, in exchange for which we had to have at least a couple of Italian actors in the cast. "Why not Christopher Lee for the part?" I said. "He's absolutely right for it and certainly most bankable." Only later did John confess to me that they had not sent my fax which they feared was too strongly worded, but the point of it was cer-tainly made, and, a few weeks later, Christopher turned up in Jaipur to play the role. Rossano Brazzi had to make do with the role of the evil, old Rana. The other Italian turned out to be a delightful lady who appeared in a dinner party scene shot in England. She had one line which had to be dubbed later because of her Italian accent. Brazzi had to be dubbed as well, and the job was done by David de Keyser, who had had previous experience of turning Brazzi's Italian

FOUR ACES: Four of the film world's most versatile and distinguished male stars are major players in the HBO PREMIERE FILMS™ mini-series THE FAR PAVILIONS, which debuts SUNDAY, APRIL 22, at 8:00 p.m. (ET) on HBO. Clockwise from top left, Omar Sharif portrays an Indian court member who becomes the friend and protector of the film's hero, Ashton Pelham-Martyn (Ben Cross); John Gielgud, a British officer caught in the conflict of the Second Afghan War; Christopher Lee, the uncle of a beautiful Indian princess (Amy Irving), and Rossano Brazzi, the omnipotent Rana of Bhithor, a feared ruler. **HBO**

The stars of *The Far Pavilions.*

delivery into passable English.

We spent Christmas in Jaipur. Ben Cross expressed his opinion that the only reason that he had not gotten an Oscar for his role in *Chariots of Fire*, which did extremely well that year, was that the Academy would also have had to give one to Ian Charleson, who played the other leading role in the film. He also implied that he intended to act Omar Sharif off the screen. I made no comment, but it did not augur well.

When actors arrive to commence work on a production, the first trial they have to endure is a make-up test and wardrobe check. This is particularly important on a costume piece like *The Far Pavilions*. I was sitting in the gardens of the palace, which was our production base, discussing some problem or other with my assistant director, when a flustered and worried make-up artist appeared and announced that we had a problem with Rossano who was adamant that he would not be made up with the beard and moustache he needed to play an Indian rajah. I went in to the make-up department fearing a major confrontation. Rossano stood there in his costume, looking rather like a doorman at a provincial curry restaurant. I asked him politely what the problem was. He wanted to be recognizable as Brazzi, he announced, not heavily disguised. This was clearly a case of actor's vanity. I picked up a reference book and showed him pictures of various Indian potentates of the nineteenth century, all

Koda Dad (Omar Sharif) and Ash (Ben Cross.

with luxurious beards, and suggested that we might perhaps just try it and then see what he felt. He agreed with some reluctance, and I left the make-up department to it. I waited in the gardens with some anxiety. Many bigger problems were at hand, and this was not a welcome extra one by any means. Some time later I was called back into the make-up room where Rossano stood surveying himself in the mirror. He actually looked rather pleased with the effect. "How do you feel now?" I asked. "Notta bad, it looksa good," he replied, stroking his false beard. I expressed my delight with his decision and heaved a sigh of relief. That problem at least was solved.

The further problem of dubbing his Italian accent would

not have to be faced until we got into post-production, and that was some months away. I don't think he was particularly happy with the demands that the role made on him, however. Getting up and down from the howdah on his regal elephant for the wedding filled him with terror. When he was carried to his funeral pyre—his last shot in the film— he would not put on his costume and, under the coverings, he was still garbed in sports jacket and Gucci shoes, hoping perhaps for a quick getaway after the end of filming.

The cameras turned over in January. From the first day of shooting, I knew that working with Jack Cardiff and his team was going to be trouble free. Jack never reminded me of the fact he had directed twelve movies himself, and

Rossano Brazzi in his "notta bad" costume
with the Maharajah of Jaipur.

we worked together in total partnership. When Jack sadly passed away in 2009, the *New York Times* obituary mentioned Jack's interest in painting—in the chiaroscuro of Caravaggio, the use of light and shadow in the work of Rembrandt, and the Impressionists' love of colour, which was such a great influence on his work. None of the obits I have read, however, mentions that Jack was also a keen painter in the Impressionist style. I never actually saw any of his work, but he showed me photographs of his paintings when we relaxed in the hotel in Jaipur after a hard day's work in the Rajasthan desert. We often chatted, too, about his fascinating experiences working with some of the great names in the movie business. I remember one funny story about *The African Queen*. When the water purification system broke down one day, the whole unit went sick—with the exception of John Huston and Humphrey Bogart, neither of whom would think of drinking water, let alone diluting their Scotch with it.

On day one, we started in the Rajasthan desert with shots of the wedding procession, using around a thousand extras. Bob Laing had done all the necessary research, and in his drawing offices I had seen detailed and meticulous sketches of how such a procession would be organized. At the head of it, a big man would sit on an elephant and beat a massive drum, which would set the pace for the soldiers' cavalry and bandsmen. Immediately behind him, on another elephant, sat an enormous wrestler, symbolizing the power of the kingdom. Nobles and dignitaries would also ride elephants, then the brides in their howdah with attendant lords and servants and finally, on foot, women servants and other menials, camp followers and animals. Raymond and his crew had started at some God-forsaken hour of the morning getting all the extras in costume. Bob's team had also been busy getting the elephants kitted out with their ornate trappings and their painted faces. Armourers and property masters were hard at work dishing out swords, lances, spears and weird musical instruments. The activity was awe-inspiring, and I could only marvel at the cool efficiency with which everything was coming together. By 9:30 in the morning, the enormous procession was all lined up in the traditional order, scrupulously observed. For the opening shot we absolutely needed a crane, but, believe it or not, the budget would not allow me one. Jack's crew managed with great ingenuity to make a primitive but effective crane-like structure out of scaffolding that, whilst it did not have the flexibility of the real thing, did at least enable us to have some fluidity of camera movement and that gave us the shot we wanted.

We were ready to turn over—"Slate one . . . Take one" —I was about to give the okay to get the wagons rolling— now's my moment to play John Ford, I thought—when one of the extras broke ranks to have a pee. We all fell about laughing but as soon as the chap, not in the least embarrassed, returned to his place, I signaled "Action!"

The Wedding Procession.

The drummer started his mighty beat and the procession got under way. My second unit crew, under Abel Goodman, were also picking up shots of parts of the procession, which on that first day would go round and round in a large circle while we filmed. Up on a nearby hill, Ash Pelham-Martin (Ben Cross) arrives, with his servant leading the packhorse, and looks down on the huge wedding procession, which is signaled to a halt. From it a solitary rider approaches and gallops across the desert to greet him. It is Omar Sharif as Koda Dad, Ash's spiritual father when he was a child in Gulkote. I held the long shot for as long as possible. I couldn't re-produce the lucky break of a mirage that made Omar's arrival so spectacular in David Lean's epic *Lawrence of Arabia*, but I hoped for some little resonance with the audience when they saw it. I am sure that Omar himself got the reference. Later he said I reminded him of David Lean in the way I approached the filming, which I suspected to be a calculated bit of flattery, but I did not mind in the least. If David Lean was not sure how he wanted to mount a scene, Omar told me, he would go out into the desert with his leading actors and talk through the problems, perhaps for two or three days. I did not have that sort of luxury. It had often been said that Lean was a perfectionist; to which my answer was that he was no more a perfectionist than I was: he simply had more time. So when I was particularly pushed on *Pavilions*, I would turn to Omar and say, "What would David do now, Omar? I haven't got three days to ponder the problem: I've only got thirty minutes to shoot the scene."

I wish I could say that my two romantic leads were also a pleasure to work with. They were not. And they were no more popular with their fellow actors than they were with me and the crew. The night John Gielgud arrived in Jaipur, I was working on the next day's shooting and could not have dinner with him. The associate producer, John Peverall, looked after him, and over dinner Sir John asked about the two leading actors. Peverall, who was as weary as I was with them, said, "Alright, but they think they know it all." "Oh," Sir John replied. "So soon?"

Being a film extra is almost a profession in all the major film making centers of the Western world. If you shoot a film in Pinewood, say, you can be pretty sure that all the extras hired for crowd scenes will be experienced at the work and know how to behave in front of the camera, never, for example, looking at the lens, knowing that when a scene is being filmed they should look animated, react as required to dramatic action, mime talking to each other if appropriate, aware that background chatter will be recorded separately after the scene is shot, with the principal characters' dialogue recorded with no background interference and the "rhubarb" added to the scene in the cutting rooms. Some extras earn themselves additional money by playing waiters or taxi drivers or whatever with the odd line of dialogue of the "Good morning, sir" or "Thank you, madam" thrown in. The reliable ones get known and regularly employed in these small parts. One chap called Vic was regularly employed at Pinewood as a particularly reliable maitre d'hotel to usher the stars to their restaurant tables with great professional flair. As he was so dependable, I decided on one occasion to give him a small role as a police inspector with half a dozen lines of written dialogue. This turned out to be a big mistake. Vic, now feeling that he was a supporting actor and not just an extra, was disastrously nervous, and I had to do take after take as he kept blowing his lines. It was not a mistake I made again. Stunt men, on the other hand, were quite a different proposition. One could give them the odd extemporized line and they had no problem with the acting. Perhaps because their relationship with the actors was of a different order.

Shooting on location in foreign countries, work is much more difficult. Often extras with little or no experience of film making have to be recruited from the local population, and for the director and his assistants life can be made irksome. One little chap dancing around in a nightclub scene in *England Made Me* somehow or other always got riveted *to* the spot right in front of the camera just when we needed to reveal Peter Finch sitting at a table on the edge of the dance floor. Neither I nor my assistant director being fluent in Serbo Croat, it took several takes and increasing exasperation from Peter before we finally managed to get the message home to the poor fellow that he really should keep moving in the approved Victor Sylvester style.

In India the problems of communication seemed even more difficult. The unwanted extras, birds and monkeys, would start chattering or chirping as the camera started to roll. One particular yellowhammer, we were sure, seemed to follow us around everywhere in the Rajasthan desert and would start on cue as we turned over the camera. My assistant director found the answer to him by firing a handgun just before each take, which always shut him up. Then an endearing old gharry driver, sitting at the reins of a stationary carriage carrying Ben Cross and Jennifer

Kendal, would start a loud rheumy coughing in the middle of a dialogue take. But the biggest problem was getting a small group of extras, who had probably never worked in front of a camera in their lives before, to act naturally within the requirements of the scene, the sort of job that the professional film extras took in their stride.

I remember a scene where a group of soldiers were sitting around a camp fire chatting with Art Malik, who played Omar Sharif's son. Our Indian assistant director explained to them what the scene was about, but they were nervous and tongue-tied, and, although Art did his best to get something out of them, the scene was just not working. It was absolutely dead. Then I had an idea. Get them, I said to the assistant director, to tell mother-in-law jokes. That worked wonderfully and the next take was perfect. It seems the mother-in-law theme is an international one.

When Omar arrived at the Rambagh Hotel, he immediately became the centre of a court of admirers. Charm was something that Omar possessed in great measure, and the hotel staff fell over themselves to please him. The Rambagh was not noted for the quality of its cuisine, but Omar soon managed to do something about that, and the quality of the curries improved tremendously. Every evening Omar and his attendant lords would sit around the tables in the dining room, and the wine would flow and all was well. The local stuff was quite undrinkable, and the cost of an imported bottle was high, so I hate to think what Omar's bar bill was by the end of his stay, because he was always generous in the extreme, and nobody else was picking up the tab. Christopher and he also got on tremendously well, and filming with both of them was relaxed and flowed easily. On one occasion Christopher was holding forth on something or other a little way from us while I was discussing a problem with Omar, which actually involved Christopher as well. Omar turned and called to him, "Christopher, could you interrupt yourself for a moment and join us" in a gently mocking tone, which Christopher took in good part.

All actors love the close-up, and some get offended if they feel the director has not done them justice in this respect in whatever scene is being shot. Often, therefore, a wise director will take close-ups of his leading stars even when he knows he may actually interrupt the flow of the action by using them. I was shooting what is called a three-handed scene where Ash is talking to the commander of the Gulkote forces and Koda-Dad stands between them, listening to what they are saying. I did a master shot of all three of them and then the conventional close shots on the two actors who had the lines that carried the scene. I then started to set up a close shot on Omar who stopped me by saying "you don't really need a close shot on me, do you Peter? Please don't waste your time on it." Thankful for his consideration, I moved on to the next sequence. But, of course, Omar also knew that the other two ac-

Enjoying a joke with Christopher and Omar.

tors had to move off out of shot, leaving him to hold the screen so in a sense he got his close-up anyway.

The wedding procession would have to travel through other chosen locations on its way to the imaginary city of Bhithor, which meant a huge organizational problem. I developed a great fondness for our team of some twenty elephants who stayed with us throughout a large part of the shoot, even when they had days off. I usually managed to take them the odd bun or two from the breakfast canteen wagons and, in the evening after a tiring day's filming, I was always pleased as my driver passed the row of them standing solemnly, waving their trunks and sometimes a jumbo foot, beautifully backlit in the soft wonderful Rajasthan sunsets. On the way back to Jaipur, I would relax in the back of the car and listen to Mozart concert arias on a Sony Walkman, and even now if I hear those particular works, I cannot avoid the odd juxtaposition in my mind of the Rajasthan desert, the elephants and the music of my favorite composer.

Having shot the sequences at the Amber Palace, we began filming at the Palace in Jaipur itself where the wedding was to take place. During this time, Steven Spielberg turned up on a location recce for his next Indiana Jones movie, *Indiana Jones and the Temple of Doom*. Accompanying him was my old friend Bob Watts who had been associate producer on *Inside Out*. Amy Irving was engaged to Steven at that time, and as I was not needing her on set for a day or two, she was able to accompany Steven on his search for locations. He turned up on my location one day after seeing the Amber Palace and said to me, "I know you are a good director because all the setups which I wanted to use, Amy said you had already used them." It was nice of him, but no English director, I thought, would express himself with such self-confidence and sound so patronizing—although I don't think for one moment that Steven intended it that way. More likely, one would get, "You bastard! Everywhere I wanted to shoot, you've already done a set-up!" or words to that effect.

The wedding sequence, shot in and around the Jaipur Palace, was one of the most visually sumptuous scenes in the movie. Raymond had designed gorgeous costumes from rich and varied fabrics for the princes and nobles in the Rana's cortege, and I would have liked to linger on each of them: one family, for example, where father and sons of different ages (from the haughty teenage prince to the diminutive little fellow of four or five), were all garbed in the same beautiful outfits. Rossano Brazzi was at the head of the cortege in his Maharajah's howdah escorted by the cavalry regiment dressed in military costume of the period, armed with sword shield and lance. Meanwhile, the two young brides were elsewhere, in an inner room of the palace being bathed, anointed and groomed for the ordeal, Anjuli looking pretty sick about the whole affair.

It all looked absolutely splendid as the procession en-

Kaka-ji and Ash arrive at the palace of the Rana of Bithor—actually the Amber Palace at Jaipur.

tered the main gates of the Palace, and the elephant arrived at the steps where Rossano would descend to be greeted by Christopher Lee and the other dignitaries of the brides' party. In the courtyard, all of the women sat cross-legged awaiting the arrival of the bridegroom, uniformly dressed in saris of bright orange red that is an old established custom. The love-sick Ash in full dress Guides uniform is forced to watch the wedding ceremony from a balcony overlooking the Palace courtyard. Presiding over the wedding ritual we had a real Brahmin priest. Everything was done with a meticulous attention to detail and accuracy.

At the end of the second Afghan War in 1879, a small force of Guides, led by Sir Louis Cavagnari as British Resident, entered Kabul and forced the Shah to sign a treaty with the British. This event is immortalized for posterity by a wonderful photograph of the parties concerned sitting outside the ceremonial tent in which the agreement was ratified. We reproduced the look of this photograph as accurately as possible. Disaster then overtook the British force when the Afghan army mutinied because they weren't getting paid, and for some obscure reason blamed it on the British. The mutineers stormed the British Residency. The Guides put up a heroic resistance but were all killed in the action. This event was a major part of the plot of Molly Kaye's novel and a big action sequence in the film.

The budget did not provide me with a military advisor,

John Gielgud as Sir Louis Cavagnari

and I could hardly expect the stunt director to be a military historian, so it was down to me to choreograph some sort of believable action. Fortunately I had read quite a lot about nineteenth century warfare, so I made a fair stab at it, although I made at least one glaring mistake in having the men march into the Residency in columns of three, instead of (as it should have been) columns of four. But I haven't so far had any angry letters from experts on the subject. To start, I got Bob Lang's team to make me a small cardboard model of the palace at Samod where we were shooting the sequence and which had various strong gates leading into the innermost courtyard. I then decided how many of the defenders should fall at each stage of the battle until a mere handful of men was left when the last stand was made. It was all great fun to shoot, but keeping the enthusiastic local extras performing the right actions presented quite a problem to the stunt director's department. A squad of Guides, under the command of Wally Hamilton, alias Benedict Taylor, waited facing the main gates. The insurgents were hammering on them with a great battering ram. Other Guides were manning the walls either side of the main gate to the interior of the Residency. As they burst open the gates, the Afghans rushed in to be faced with a withering volley of fire from the front line of Wally's platoon, which then, in correct military fashion, moved back through the ranks to allow the second rank to fire while they reloaded. Rather well conceived, I thought.

The only trouble was that the crowd bursting through the gates got over enthusiastic and rushed forward so fast without any "casualties," so the whole effect of the shot was ruined. In order to stop this gadarene rush, I had the doorway blocked with barrels and casks so that their progress was immediately halted, while the ones who had been instructed to fall down dead did so and the others had to open fire from the gate area. Take Two—and this time all went well. Wally's men retired in good order, taking the Union Jack with them through the inner gates, drawing their sabres in splendid fashion and fighting a rearguard action before shutting the great doors behind them.

In the next stage of the action, Ash, who, disguised as a tribesman, had been mingling with the mutineers in the streets of the city, sees the attack commence and rides off to collect a mounted foraging party. They gallop in through the gates, the idea being that they dismount and fight their way through the enemy to get inside the inner sanctum with the others. This time the shot went wrong for a different reason. The Guides galloped in and then did not get off their horses but just milled around in an aimless way. An exasperated assistant director sent by a despairing director to ask *what the hell was going on* found out the reason was that the horsemen, who had been lent to us by the local Indian cavalry regiment, were afraid that some harm might come to their horses and were reluctant to leave go of them. The plot had to be explained to them carefully for the second time, and finally they got the message and we got the shot.

The Cavalry Regiment had agreed to help us whenever we needed them, but they were not always reliable. I had dreamt up another John Ford type shot: when the procession gets near Gulkote, they suddenly see a row of sinister-looking horsemen on the hilltop before them. We set up to shoot it, but the cavalry had not arrived. We waited and they still did not turn up, so in the end I had to make do with a much smaller contingent of horsemen. Sadly I did not quite achieve the look of Geronimo and the Apache about to attack John Wayne and the Seventh Cavalry that I had hoped for.

Our scratch cricket team often played matches against the Regiment, which we inevitably lost even though I wore my MCC tie to the games. It was rumored that our opponents had imported one or two county level players to ensure victory, but I don't think they need have bothered. In one match, Omar, who was having trouble with his leg, had to get my teenage son, who was "gophering" on the movie, to run for him, although I don't think he had to do so more than once or twice. Saeed, however, did confuse the opposition with his bowling a series of remarkable "donkey-drops," which to everyone's surprise earned him a wicket or two.

The climax of *The Far Pavilions* takes place at the funeral of the wicked old Rana of Bithor where Shushila, who

Shushila (Sneh Gupta) about to become suttee
on her husband's funeral pyre.

has surprisingly actually begun to love her husband, goes
to *become suttee* and, as was expected of widows, to
die in the flames of her husband's funeral pyre. This was a
royal custom and privilege that classical writers mentioned
as early as 316 BC, but it later became more general. Any
woman who refused to perform it was ostracized.

The British abolished the custom in 1829, but it still
took place until quite recent times in the more remote
parts of India. The setting for the funeral ceremony had to
be a chattri. These were memorial sites raised on the spot
where the rulers' bodies were burned. Many such ruins
may be seen across Rajastan, "vast empty tombs" as Molly

Kaye describes them, "built of the local sandstone and intricately and beautifully carved, some of them three and four stories high so that their airy domed pavilions stand above the tree tops." Finding such a magnificent location near to Jaipur was not difficult. The real problem for my team was assembling a great concourse of white dhoti-clad extras to witness the event. It was our suspicion that many of them believed that they were watching the real thing, and I can only say that they behaved wonderfully, with great solemnity and dignity and sense of occasion. Thankfully, this time, nobody decided that he needed to take a leak just before the cameras began to roll. Once again, we had to take great care in getting the details right: the way in which the widow is taken into a small temple building to be ritually divested of richly bejeweled ornaments before making her last walk to the funeral pyre, the chanting of the priests and the responses from the watching crowds. The Brahmin priest who had officiated at the wedding of the two sisters was with us, and so I could be confident that the religious aspects of the ceremony would be correctly observed. For the long shots of the actual burning, the camera crew had set up a clever system that reflected flames into the camera lens over the image of the funeral pyre so that it appeared to burn, although, in fact, at this point of the filming it was not actually alight, for we could not afford to set fire to it until we went in for close shots. The time and effort needed to set it up again if anything went wrong and we needed a second take were out of the question. The filming went extraordinarily well. Ash shoots Shushila at the moment she realizes what is happening to her and terror overwhelms her as the flames take over from her exalted state of mourning. Ash, Anjuli and their followers make good their escape from the scene, pursued by Bhitor horsemen who are then routed in a rear guard ambush led by Koda Dad and Ash, while Anjuli is taken on to safety. Koda Dad gets mortally wounded in the action, and Omar had a rather long death speech to deliver to the heartbroken Ashton Pelham-Martin. When we turned over, a group of monkeys who were among the bystanders decided to have an argument about something or other and ruined the soundtrack of an otherwise perfect take. Naturally, the scene belonged to Omar, for he had to carry the dialogue, and I had to ask him if he could bear to do it again, hopefully without the off-screen comments of the bloody monkeys. Omar, as always the perfect professional, said no problem. However, Ben Cross decided to object on the basis that he had given his emotional all, and what did I expect from him again? Could we perhaps provide an onion to bring the tears to his eyes that the scene demanded? A party of journalists from the English papers happened to be there to witness the shooting of this sequence, and so to my acute embarrassment, they overheard Ben's outburst. The only action to take was to ignore it and push on with take two, which is what we did, and, we did. Fortunately, the monkeys kept quiet this time—maybe because they, too, were embarrassed, or more likely because some members of the crew had frightened them off.

Filming completed in Jaipur, we moved on to shoot our last few sequences in Delhi before returning home to some weeks of studio work in England. The schedule on the *Pavilions* being fairly long, the Indian tax laws made it necessary for the entire crew to be out of the country for a couple of days during the filming. I chose to go to Katmandhu, and Jack took over directing for the two days I was there. I don't know if we had the same shooting style, or if Jack adapted to mine, but the sequences he directed for me fitted seamlessly into my work. In Delhi, we did a romantic two shot of Ben Cross and Amy Irving against an evening sunset on a small hillock, ignoring the fact that we were beside the main road into the city with the traffic roaring beneath us.

We were scheduled to leave on a flight at some ungodly hour of the morning and, after a party in the hotel at which some members of the crew and cast drank rather more than they should have done, I went off for a farewell dinner with our unit doctor, Sudhir Krishna. On my return, having said goodbye to Sudhir, who then drove off to his home some distance away, I entered the hotel foyer to be greeted by an anxious American hippy type whom we had co-opted onto the wardrobe unit. "Thank God you are back," she said. "Ben 's OD'd!" I followed her up to

Ben's room where several younger members of the cast and crew were standing around looking helpless. When I left for dinner, Ben had already drunk quite a bit, but since then, it seemed, he had unwisely taken some sort of cocktail of drugs, and he was stretched out on the floor of the room, his complexion an odd colour indeed. They had tried to ring Krishna, but he was, of course, not at home as he had been out at dinner with me, and so far all attempts to contact the hotel doctor had failed.

I rang the associate producer's room, and his girlfriend said he was in bed. I said John had better get down as quickly as possible because it looked to me as if we might be faced with a crisis, which could mean total disaster for the movie. Rupert Everett was among those present and, as he seemed to be more or less in charge of the situation, I asked him if any odd substances were about in the room. He knew, of course, exactly what I meant and I suggested a little cleaning up might be in order. Eventually the hotel doctor arrived, made a quick diagnosis and arranged for an ambulance to take Ben to hospital as soon as possible. Sudhir arrived back as the ambulance drove off and followed after it. John and I were worried when the hotel doctor said that, in his opinion, Mr. Cross was in a very serious condition, and whether or not he survived depended on how strong his constitution was. We finally boarded our plane for home uncertain as to whether or not we still had an important actor alive. No doubt—without him the film could not be completed.

Fortunately for us—and especially for him—he had a strong constitution. As soon as they arrived at the hospital, Sudhir immediately pumped out of his stomach a lethal mixture of God knows what. Ben was able to join us at Twickenham Studios a couple of days later for the last three weeks of the schedule.

Our final scenes were shot in Snowdonia in Wales with Cross and Irving. Now happily reunited with his childhood sweetheart Anjuli, Ash rides off with her towards the Himalayan mountains—the far pavilions—or more truthfully, Mount Snowdonia, behind which the film laboratories cleverly superimposed a still photograph of the real thing taken by our unit photographer, David James. Immediately after the last shot was in the can, Amy rushed off to London without saying goodbye to anyone. She had to meet Steven Spielberg at Heathrow Airport, and it was reported she turned up there covered in gold paint as a consolation to Steven who had not won an Oscar at the recent ceremonies in Hollywood, but this may just have been a rumour.

So now we were in for ten weeks hard work in the cutting rooms at Twickenham Studios with my editor, Johnny Jympson, and his team. The plan was to make a cinema feature film at the same time out of the material we shot for the mini-series. This was a common practice at the time, but it never worked satisfactorily. Television is largely a medium with much more dialogue than used in a movie, and this applies to the mini-series with all its pretensions to be like a feature film spread over several evenings of viewing. Lots of television airtime had to be filled, and the way to fill it was with plenty of dialogue scenes—hopefully good ones—which is not the case with most movies, even those which are not pure action pieces. If the intention is to make a cinema movie at the same time as the mini-series, then a separate script should be written to cinema length and, where necessary, scenes must be shot in two versions. This, of course, implies a great deal of extra shooting time, probably not allowed for in the original budget and schedule. So what usually happened was that all you got was a seriously edited down version of the original piece in which much of the original story was lost, and the result might even become incomprehensible in places. Johnny and I slaved away for a long time to produce a short version of the story, nipping and tucking, cutting bits of dialogue here and there while maintaining a coherent story line and losing none of the spectacular scenes that gave the film its glossy, big budget look.

We produced a version running a little over two hours that Jake Eberts at Goldcrest was happy with. I went away for a two week skiing holiday in France. When I returned, I found that the Goldcrest salesman had said that it was too long to be sold to cinema distributors (who had to have so many showings a day to make a profit) with the result that a particularly atrocious hatchet job had been done.

In the process, John Gielgud's character had been completely cut out of the picture, although one of the reasons for having John in the film in the first place was because he was a good "marquee name." The Kabul episode was reduced to a sort of border skirmish. Fortunately the film was not shown in England at all, only in far off lands.

The Far Pavilions got excellent viewing figures on its first run on UK television, and some of the senior executives at Channel Four treated themselves to a splendid weekend somewhere or other to celebrate the event. I flew to Los Angeles to attend a big cinema showing HBO had arranged and stayed with Christopher Lee and his wife, Gitte, who were living on Wilshire Boulevard at the time. Certainly on its second television showing in the UK, *The Far Pavilions* achieved much better figures than the arguably more serious offering *The Jewel in the Crown*. But not everybody at Channel Four felt the same way. An aspiring young Indian film producer had sent me a rather indifferent script which I had politely acknowledged but did not intend to pursue. He had at the same time sent the script, with my name attached to his application for finance, to one Farrukh Dhondy who ran an Asian department at Channel Four. Mr. Dhondy replied that he did not like *The Far Pavilions* one bit and thought it was "in monstrously bad taste" and so, he said, did many of the editorial team at C4. He added that if he had had anything to do with it, they would not have transmitted it. Clearly it offended Mr.

Dhondy's view of what was politically correct, and company loyalty was not going to prevent him from saying so. The full television version was shown in India where apparently audiences loved it. I was happy when Saeed, who was still commuting to Bollywood, told me that a distinguished Indian film director had said to him that it was a pity that Indian cinema could not realize the days of the British Raj as accurately as we had. Obviously I prefer his view to that of the egregious Mr. Farrukh Dhondy.

The She Wolves

Much of my film education had been in the art house cinemas of London. I learnt to love the French cinema through afternoons and evenings spent in the Everyman in Hampstead and the Academy in Oxford Street. There I saw wonderful actors like Louis Jouvet and Michel Simon, Jules Berry and Jean Gabin, Arletty, Fernandel and many others in classics of French Cinema like *Le Jour se Leve*, *Hotel Du Nord*, *Carrefour*, *La Grande Illusion*, *Les Visiteurs du Soir* and the legendary Gerard Philippe in Claude Autant-Lara's *Le Diable au Corps*. I loved the work of great directors like Jean Renoir, Henri Clouzot, Jacques Feyder, who made the wonderful *La Kermesse Heroique* with Francoise Rosay, and Marcel Carne, whose *Les Enfants du Paradis* remains one of my favorite movies of all time. This film never ages however many times one sees it. Later, of course, came the New Wave of French cinema challenging the traditions.

So when the opportunity to make a film in France came my way, I leapt at it. The script was adapted from *Les*

Louves, a novel by two French thriller writers, Boileau and Narcejac, famous for *Les Diaboliques,* which was made into a classic *film noir* by Henri Clouzot. It had, like much of their work, a series of plot twists of Byzantine complexity. Two French POWs in World War II named Bernard and Gervais manage to escape from a prison camp and plan to make their way to Lyon, home of Helene who has been writing in friendly fashion to Bernard, whom she has never actually met and whom he believes will give them sanctuary. Then, in an encounter with German soldiers in the Lyon railway yards, Bernard is run over by a train and fatally injured. His friend Gervais escapes and makes his way to the home of the woman in question, who is one of two sisters in reduced circumstances making a living teaching piano. The sisters think he is the dead man—or so it seems—and he goes along with the deception. Then the plot gets complicated, a number of surprise twists occur and all ends rather nastily with both sisters coming to a sticky end. The film was to be made as an Anglo-French co-production and shot in two languages, which demanded a bilingual cast. The main challenge for us was to make a film that would not be what Jeremy Isaacs, then head of Channel Four Television that was partly financing the project, wittily called a "Euro-pudding." Quite a few co-productions being made at that time fell into this category: films without a true national character, actors speaking in a variety of accents and so on.

Cherie Lunghi as Helene.

I felt I had to try and make the film with a genuine French atmosphere and avoid the kind of synthetic feel that Jeremy was criticizing. We had Cherie Lunghi as the scheming woman who becomes a murderess, Andrea Ferreol as the sister of the dead man, the beautiful, young Mathilde May, in her first major speaking role, as Cherie's younger sister, Yves Beneyton as the surviving POW Gervais and Ralph Bates as Bernard, his co-escaper who dies in the rail yard. Every dialogue scene had to be shot in both English and French, which sometimes produced comical moments when the actors got mixed up, and I had to cut the shot and remind them which version we were actually shooting.

Lyon was a famous centre of the Resistance during the Nazi Occupation. The notorious Klaus Barbie headed up the Gestapo presence there, and he trapped the great Resistance hero, Jean Moulin, whose name is honoured in streets and squares in every city in France. The old town—the setting for our story—is a honeycomb of tiny streets and alleyways between the main streets known as *traboules*, which were of great assistance to the men and women of the Resistance who could disappear easily into the rabbit warren of houses and apartments therein. The setting was atmospheric, and I worked hard to re-create the colour of the times: the queues for food, the sudden knocking on doors late at night, the demand for papers of identification on street corners, the mood of terror and suspicion, and the presence of German agents and sol-diers on the streets.

After a short sequence on a little steam-railway run-ning between Chinon and Richelieu, we moved to Paris for the studio shooting of interiors. The studio we used was situated at Joinville in the east suburbs of Paris. It was getting "past its sell-by date" and due to be shut down. I liked to think that, in the past, some of the great stars of French cinema had also worked on the same stages that we were now using. It turned out that Andréa Ferréol, a big star of the current French cinema, was close to my old friend Omar Sharif, and for me a great delight was to dine with them and Cherie Lunghi, who had recently worked

Andrea Ferreol and Gervais (Yves Beneyton.)

with Omar and Jeanne Moreau in a television version of Jean Paul Sartre's play *Huit Clos*. Omar lived in a grandiose apartment in a posh arrondissement and, with his usual generosity, was able to offer Cherie her own room there during shooting. Ralph Bates and I also struck up a close friendship, which survived the end of the shooting when a mutual love of cricket found us together at Lord's Test Matches, and he did appear in another movie that I made. Sadly, Ralph died a few years later of pancreatic cancer. He was greatly missed by his family and many friends.

Unlike our own practice when shooting starts at around 8:30 in the morning, the French have a more civilized way of going about things. Shooting starts after lunch and goes on without a break until 8:00 in the evening. That way, they argue, the women always look at their best because they don't have to get to the studio at an ungodly hour for make-up. French crews were marvelous, too. They all seemed to have a total passionate dedication to the cinema, and one could discuss movies intelligently with the stagehands as well as the leading technicians.

Helene, the role played by Cherie Lunghi, scraped a living in wartime Lyons by teaching the piano. I spent some time looking for piano works that would be dramatically right for the film and, to my great joy, found a work that I had not known before. It came at the end of a great series of piano sonatas by Haydn, which I had owned on record for some time but had not fully explored. It was his extraordinarily dramatic *Seven Last Words from the Cross*, which he had originally composed as a choral work commissioned by the Bishop of Cadiz. He then reworked it both as a string quartet and also as an extended sonata-like work for piano. I used that as background music for the titles, which were played out against scenes of Cherie walking across the Square in the old town and then segued to her sitting at the piano in the apartment that she shared with her sister (Mathilde May), and later in the film I used the composer string quarter version.

I had a fine French composer, Raymond Alessandrini, writing the score. We also had the problem of finding some young French kids who could play piano to be in various

Helene (Cherie Lunghi) plays Haydn's *Seven Last Words*.

scenes where we saw Helene somewhat wearily teaching them. Raymond taught at the Paris Conservatoire, and he lined up a number of young boys and girls to audition for me. I was quite moved watching these incredibly talented young people play, and so choosing from them the ones I would have play in my film proved difficult. I had a great rapport with Raymond and was able to use him to score two other films for me.

During the Paris filming, I stayed at L'Abbaie, one of my favorite little hotels on the Left Bank, and I could stroll down to St. Germain to get my newspaper and repair for a leisurely breakfast of coffee and croissants at the Deux Magots or the Cafe Flore. My friend Bob Parrish, the American director, originally recommended me to L'Abbaie. He had stayed there for the first time when he was in Paris with an American Army film unit. It was his favorite hotel in Paris, and it became mine too. Bob also introduced me to the French director, Bertrand Tavernier, whom I had much wanted to meet after seeing *Round Midnight*, his superb film about jazz. Bob had known Bertrand when he was a critic for *Cahiers*, the French film journal, and Bob and he had made, as a labour of love, a documentary film called *Mississippi Blues*. Later I was able to invite Bertrand to London for a showing of one of his films at the National Film Theatre, followed by an on-stage talk. The Directors Guild had organized a series of events for which one film director talked to another about his work. We ran *Une Semaine de Vacances*, and I talked to Bertrand about his movies. Michael Powell turned up, having been an old friend of Tavernier, and it was a great pleasure to meet the legendary director. At the drinks session after the show, I introduced Bertrand to an old friend of mine, who had a much loved cat he called Lester after the great saxophonist, Lester Young. "Anybody who has a cat called Lester can't be all bad," said Bertrand.

The composers that I have worked with whose work I found most sympathetic were Raymond, Mike Westbrook and John Scott, who did the score for *England Made Me*. John had been slated to do *The Far Pavilions*, but because David Puttnam had not liked his score for *Experi-*

With Michael Powell and Bertrand Tavernier
at the National Film Theatre in London.

ence Preferred and got it rewritten by another composer, Geoff Reeve decided to dump and replace him. As Geoff had signed John in the first place, Geoff clearly should have explained to him what had happened, but unfortunately he didn't do so. For a long time, John's feeling that in some way I had betrayed him made relations between us rather awkward. Then the rift was healed some years later when John was able to do the score for me for a children's film called *The King of the Wind.*

Back to the Woodstock Road

From my days up at Oxford, I do not remember mur-
ders happening in university circles as frequently
as they do in Colin Dexter's highly enjoyable *Inspector
Morse* detective stories, but to go back to my old *alma
mater* to shoot one of the television adaptations was a
great pleasure.

"Last Bus to Woodstock" was actually the first of the
Inspector Morse novels, but not the first to be filmed by
a long way. Woodstock is a small village eight miles north
of Oxford and famous for Blenheim Palace, birthplace of
Winston Churchill, which is now open to the public. A bus
service runs from the centre of Oxford that goes down the
Woodstock Road, where I actually had lodgings during
my second year at university.

Michael Cox wrote the adaptation and made many
important changes to the plot line. He dropped some
of the seedier aspects of the story and characters that,
in the eighties, were felt to be unsuitable for prime time
TV audiences. The story centers on the death of a pretty

young girl Sylvia Kane in the car park of a pub, the Fox and Castle in Woodstock. She has last been seen waiting in the heavy rain with another girl, at an Oxford to Woodstock bus stop, by an elderly widow, Mrs. Jarman. She tells Morse that the dead girl was picked up by a passing motorist, and that her friend decided to wait for the bus. In Sylvia's handbag, Morse finds a coded letter addressed to one Jennifer Coleby, a woman who works for the same financial services company as the dead girl. Before long, Morse and his Sergeant Lewis have a bewildering list of suspects of both sexes, including the young man, John Sanders, who was waiting for her in the pub, two Oxford dons, Bernard Crowther and Peter Newlove, and several others. As is often the case in murder mysteries, suspects tell many lies, some of them to cover their sexual transgressions that have nothing to do with the death of the girl in the Fox and Castle car park. "A tangled web of passion and corruption," as the *TV Times* magazine described the episode.

Cox chose cleverly to underline the sexual themes of the story with the erotic poetry of John Wilmot, Earl of Rochester. Bernard Crowther, himself an adulterer, lectures on the randy poet. Morse goes to Coleby's house to interview her and meets two other girls who share the home with her. Jennifer, played by Jill Baker, and Mary Widdowson, a nurse played by Ingrid Lacey, turn out to be both deeply involved in the central drama. Michael also changed the third member of the trio into Angie Hartman, a bright, young undergraduate studying English literature with whom Morse is able to discuss Rochester's poems. The part was nicely played by a charming young actress named Holly Aird who has since made her mark in several successful television series. Angie invites him to go with her to Bernard Crowther's lecture. Morse sits in the audience accompanied by the pretty, young undergraduate, and behind him sits Colin Dexter making his usual Hitchcock-inspired appearance in the episode. Angie, who can talk wisely about passion and lust, is a complete innocent and becomes deeply distressed when her tutor, Peter Newlove, attempts to have sex with her during a tutorial. This was another strand in the complex story of sexual relationships that made *Last Bus* more than a simple murder mystery and such an interesting story to film.

The Oxford colleges were surprisingly co-operative with the production company, unlike the situation I had encountered at "the other place" when I shot a sequence there for one of the *Racing Game* episodes. We shot around the Radcliffe Camera, in Brasenose College and outside Hertford, and in various lanes and streets in the city. I chose Worcester College as the main setting for the story, and I was able to use the lovely gardens (where Nevill Coghill set his *Tempest* production which I wrote about earlier) for a scene where Crowther confesses to his wife that it was he who picked up Sylvia at the bus stop.   The series developed Morse's love of classical music as well as his interest in crossword puzzles, and I told the composer, Barrington Phelong, that I would like to use some Mozart. We had the overture to *Cosi Fan Tutti* playing on the radio in Morse's Jaguar as he drove down Beaumont Street to interview the suspects at Worcester College. On the detective's bookshelves one could see a row of Wisden cricket almanacs indicating another interest. A later episode, however, that centered around a cricket team had Morse, in his most curmudgeonly way, expressing a deep dislike of cricket and everything to do with it!

By the time we came to shoot "Last Bus to Woodstock," John Thaw and Kevin Whately had settled well into their parts, and the director needed to do little except give them the moves and discuss any problems they might have with the script. They were both highly professional actors, and working with them was pleasant and easy.

Michael had written the part of Mrs. Jarman, the elderly lady who is a key witness, with a certain actor, a sweet lady named Fabia Drake, in mind, and I was more than happy to go along with his suggestion. Another young up-and-coming actor, Perry Fenwick, played the role of Jimmy, created by Michael, a poolroom bully and post boy at the company for whom Jennifer Coleby works. Perry now stars as Billy Mitchell, a central figure in the BBC soap opera, *East Enders.*

While writing this chapter, out of curiosity I looked up the series on the Internet and discovered some interest-

Inspector Morse (John Thaw) and Sergeant Lewis (Kevin Whateley).

ing viewer comments. One considered "Last Bus to Woodstock" to be one of the best episodes of the *Inspector Morse*
series: "Keeping both Morse and the viewer stumped until
the last moment when the dreadful truth sinks in."

The most perceptive of them commented on the sex
and gender themes rather than the plot twists. I quote
again: "Although the case is closed, there's no sense of
justice being fulfilled, only lives ruined, a little more mis-
ery in an already miserable world. The *Inspector Morse*
series never drew the nicest picture of society, but in this
episode, it seems particularly grim."

Punch magazine cartoon

Another summed up the story beautifully: "Gender roles and loneliness are the recurring themes that serve as the foundation for this visit to Oxford: Among the dozens of characters introduced, all but two live hauntingly lonely lives, coping as they may—through drinking, gambling, sex and adultery."

As it turned out, no murder has occurred, but a tragic accident borne out of passion and jealousy. As Morse and Lewis walk away from camera in the closing shot, Morse quotes Rochester:

"All this to love and rapture's due; Must we not pay a debt to pleasure too?"

Time Spent in the West Country.

My second marriage came to its end at the time I began a number of projects with HTV, a provincial company that had the franchise for the South West of England, operating out of studios in Bristol. It had a fairly good record of producing drama for the national network. Shortly after I returned from France, I was offered a script in a series of films with supernatural themes. Managing director, Patrick Dromgoole, put the co-production project together, set up with the French TV Channel Antenne 2. The producer was Peter Graham Scott who, many years before, had been a feature film editor, and his credits in that capacity included the famous Graham Greene movie, *Brighton Rock*. He had also directed feature films and a good number of TV episodes, including *The Avengers*.

The script, *Hand in Glove*, told the story of a young woman going quietly mad when her love life goes wrong. On a visit with her best friend to a country church she begins to see things, including her marriage to her ex-boyfriend and his being trampled to death by a rampaging herd of cows! She also has a weird vision of a number of sad-looking ladies in period costume on the other side of the riverbank, which rather upsets their picnic lunch. They then meet a local lady who lives in an old house near the church and tells them about the ghosts of deserted women who appear from time to time. As the unfortunate young woman Catherine, I cast Nicola Pagett, whom I had first worked with in *Man in a Suitcase*. One of the contractual obligations was the casting of at least one French actor in each film, so Catherine's sympathetic friend was played by the charming French actress Sylvie Granotier; the local lady by Trevor Howard's lovely wife Helen Cherry,and the male lead by Clive Francis, who had first worked with me on an episode of Anthony Quayle's *Strange Report*.

The story was spooky and full of opportunities to make an atmospheric film. I didn't feel happy about the idea of Clive being chased by a herd of cows. I could see great problems in trying to get some placid English cattle behaving like the bulls in Pamplona, so I changed them to horses, which do have a sexual potency in popular imagery about stallions. That worked well with the help of a most competent lady horse master, who got her splendid animals charging terrifying down the hillside.

In a night scene where the demented Catherine rises from her bed and walks slowly through the streets of Bath, I was able to get permission to use Maria Callas' beautiful recording of the aria "casta diva" from Puccini's opera *Norma*. It worked wonderfully.

The heroine dies at the end of the story, and the final scene was set in a church. Helen said to me that I should have asked Trevor to play the role of the vicar, as he would be more than happy to do it for me just to be down in Bristol with her during the filming. I had thought of it but felt that I could hardly offer him such a small part. We had already cast a local jobbing actor in the role, but when I spoke to Peter Graham Scott about Helen's suggestion, he was happy to pay off the local chap and offer it to Trevor, who turned up next morning. We had a pleasant and rather vinous dinner together, and Trevor and I commiserated over *The Honorary Consul* in which Graham Greene and I had both wanted him to play Charlie Fortnum.

The vicar has a long speech, and because Trevor had really had little time to memorize it, we set up what the industry rudely calls an "idiot's board," which is to say a board with the text large enough to be read by the actor just out of shot. Truth be told, he didn't actually need it, and in the first take got through the part with no problem whatsoever.

At this time Peter Graham Scott read my script *Flight* and wanted to do it as one of a series of low (in this case positively minuscule) budget productions. Rewrites were yet again demanded and, on Peter's suggestion, I reset the story in Berlin. Then, after he had been on holiday to Istanbul, I rewrote it yet again with the setting now the Turkish capital. I am sure that his trip then became a legitimate location recce expense.

Today, with highly organized airport security, I like to believe no one can get past the rigid security checks with a hidden bomb mechanism. At that time, security was more lax so it was just about possible, and I contrived a situation where the child offered the doll to the Turkish security policeman, but he waved it away with a friendly smile as not something he felt necessary to check, which seemed convincing enough. I also built up the role of the private investigator, giving him a background of a failed marriage of his own and a small daughter he was prevented from seeing.

Casting was now on a much less grand scale. Helen was played by Jenny Seagrove, who was in *Local Hero*. To satisfy the French co-financing distributors, we needed a French co-star, so the terrorist was played by Jean Claude Dauphin, son of the great French film star Claude Dauphin. The role of Mrs Setty was accepted by Judy Campbell, the distinguished star of English theatre and mother of Jane Birkin who became a big name in France after her hit record *Je t'aime (moi non plus)* with Serge Gainsbourg. The detective was played by Dinsdale Landen, who I felt gave the best performance in the film. For the little girl I had to use a child, Caitlin Kiddy, from an acting school set up in Bristol by HTV.

The miserable budget meant all sorts of corner cutting. In Istanbul we shot the scenes of Helen and her daughter arriving at Istanbul airport and being given a lift to their hotel by the helpful young man who turns out to be a terrorist. We shot them as Jenny and the little girl arrived at the airport from Heathrow, having put on their costumes and been made up when they got off the plane.

We shot various exteriors and street and park scenes in the city, including a boat trip up the Bosphorus.

When shooting in Turkey was complete we were due to return home to finish the film on locations around Bristol. Our plane was very late arriving at Istanbul and we sat around in the airport restaurant and lounges for a long time watching planes landing. Jenny Seagrove was, at that time, the partner of the film director Michael Winner and she spent several hours in a search to see if she could find

Helen (Jenny Seagrove) and her daughter (Caitlin Kiddy)
arriving at Istanbul Airport.

an alternative and quicker flight home to him. Night fell and we could now see little more than the landing lights. As Jenny sat down after her fruitless search, a plane was was just coming in. Dinsdale Landen (a king of one-liners) said, pointing at its landing lights, "Look, Jenny—I think Michael's on that plane. Isn't that the end of his cigar?" Laughter all around, but she was not amused.

Interiors had to be filmed in England as well as the action high points of the story—a riot outside a cinema, an assassination on a train and the final attempt to hijack a plane that had to be shot at Bristol airport. The rattle of machine gun fire, in the wee small hours, as the terrorists tried to storm the aircraft caused some panic among the sober citizens of Bristol who lived around the airport, and crew members had to be sent out to allay their fears, whilst the publicist, Ros Cliffe, who had left the set at 3 am, was immediately called back to work to deal with a number of phone calls from the press, no doubt somewhat disappointed to discover that their story was to be only a minor one.

I changed the title of the film to *Some Other Spring*, the name of a beautiful song recorded by Billie Holiday with lyrics that mirrored well the story of a doomed love affair. I tried to get permission to use the Holiday recording, but it was too expensive—unlike the situation at the BBC where there was some sort of blanket deal with the record companies that allowed me to use a Holiday track

The author and his wife Rosslyn, by the Trevi fountain in Rome.

in my adaptation of Margaret Drabble's novel, *The Waterfall*, and Sir Georg Solti's *Der Rosenkavalier* recording in *Caught on a Train*. As the commercial TV companies had to pay such high usage fees, my French music director, Raymond Alessandrini, recorded the song for me in Paris with the Scottish jazz singer, Carole Kidd, whom we took over for the session. Raymond hired a group of Paris jazz musicians, which to my delight included the fine bass player, Pierre Michelot. Pierre had played with every American jazz star who had ever recorded in Paris, and he appeared in my friend Bertrand Tavernier's film, *Round Midnight*, backing the great tenor saxist Dexter Gordon, the star of the film. By extraordinary coincidence, when we were filming the shots at Istanbul airport, who should I see going in but the jazz clarinetist Tony Scott who actually played on Billie Holiday's second recording of *Some Other Spring*. He was based in Rome at that time where I had heard him play at a nightclub, and when I spoke to him, he explained that he was on his way back there after playing a concert in Istanbul.

It was on this production that I first met the publicist Rosslyn Cliffe, who worked both on this film and on the feature film which I subsequently made for the company. Ros and I became firm friends, sharing a great love of dogs.

Back to the Front

After a long, drawn out and horribly expensive divorce, I was able to marry the lovely Rosslyn, who has made me a very happy and lucky man. After HTV, Ros worked for another television company in the south of England and then became director of fundraising and public relations for two national charities.

We spent a great deal of time at our house in Somerset in a small village called Winsham near the Dorset border. Walking through the village churchyard, I was always reminded of Wilfred Owen's poignant line:

"Trumpets calling to them from the sad shires…"

My interest in military history had found its only outlet on screen in the battle sequences of *The Far Pavilions*. I had always wanted to make a film about The Great War of 1914/18. With Rosslyn, I made a long planned trip to the battlefields of France.

A four-day visit to the Western Front is too short a time in which to take in the enormity of what happened in Flanders and Picardy during those four terrible years. Yet, in that short time, we found ourselves emotionally exhausted by the sheer weight of the sad history of this flat country where, ninety odd years after the horrible slaughters that marked it forever, the shards of the battlegrounds still come to the surface in fields and ridges.

We had planned to visit Ypres and the Somme and took with us two invaluable books: Stephen O'Shea's *Back to the Front*, the story of his amazing endurance feat of walking the whole length of the Western Front, some four hundred and fifty miles of it, from Nieuport to the Swiss frontier, and Tonie and Valmai Holt's *Battlefields of the First World War*, a less personal account but combining a concise narrative account of many major actions with practical guides and maps for daily tours of each battlefield area.

On our first night in the Ypres Salient, we stayed at Varlet Farm, an attractive farmhouse on the edge of the village Poelkapelle, close to Passchendaele, which the owners run as a successful bed and breakfast. As recently as 1999, they told us, they had unearthed in their fields a German Maxim Gun still in quite good condition. We saw this artifact in one of their barns, along with a small collection of such items which they had found over the years in their farmland. Everywhere are such small private museums. Shell cases, spent bullets, hand grenades, tin helmets, decaying scraps of gas masks and other military impedimenta are on display in barns and sheds, where the owners hope to make a little money from the war buffs and tourists. Every village has a cemetery or even two with the rows of crosses and gravestones.

Three major battles were fought in the Ypres Salient, culminating in the 1917 offensive centering on the German-held Passchendaele Ridge. On the 22nd of July in that year, Haig launched the preliminary bombardment of the German lines by some 3,000 pieces of artillery that turned the battlefields into a vast swamp in which a man who slipped off the duckboards would most certainly sink down to die in the mud and filth. Haig still believed in the fantasy of a glorious cavalry breakthrough and, as O'Shea observes, the disaster of the Somme and thirty-six months of warfare had taught him nothing. "We died in hell, they called it Passchendaele," wrote Siegfried Sassoon, and it is said that a senior staff officer named Lancelot Kiggel visited the front when the fighting was over and burst into tears, saying "Good God! Did we really send men to fight in this?" He might also have asked, "Why did we let Haig do it?"

On our first morning, we went to the enormous Tyne Cot cemetery on the Passchendaele Ridge where the names of 35,000 soldiers with no known grave are inscribed on the long white marble wall that backs the cemetery. One of our friends had told me of her uncle who had died at Passchendaele, and we had promised to look for his grave at Tyne Cot. He was a lieutenant in the Northumberland Fusiliers, who had left many men at that place. Legend has it that the Northumberland Regiment christened the ridge Tyne Cot because the German pillboxes silhouetted on the skyline reminded them of cottages at home.

But Second Lieutenant James Angus Scott had no grave. He was just one of the thousands of men listed on the wall that backs the cemetery, who in the "fortunes of war" (as the inscriptions everywhere in Flanders and Picardy put it), had been blown to bits or lost in the mud to be eaten by rats: "Denied the known and honoured burial given to their comrades in death." We found Lt. Scott's name, and I dutifully took photographs of it and the thousands of gravestones of unidentified soldiers. Perhaps one of them was his but, as the inscriptions have it, he and all the rest are known only to God. To us they are "The Missing" of the three battles of Ypres, the Somme and all the other fields of death whose names resonate in the memory: Mametz Wood, the Messines Ridge, Vimy, Cambrai, Hill 60 and so on.

Nearby was the Passchendaele Museum with the inevitable reconstruction of a section of a trench and dugouts. At a place called Hooge, am enormous mine crater may be seen in the grounds of a hotel and close by a small museum claiming to be the best private museum in Flanders. It houses among other items a copy of a German Fokker DR1 Triplane, the machine flown by the Red Baron von Richthofen and one of the war planes that I modeled as a schoolboy, along with the SE5s and Sopwith Camels.

Nearby is Sanctuary Wood, another private museum, the owner of which, Jacques Schier, would probably contest the Hooge claim to be the best. Behind it is a preserved stretch of trench on the Schier property, and it costs six euros to visit it. The entrance is through a shabby shop and cafe with Coca-Cola signs and souvenirs for sale. The owner, we gathered, is scathingly called "Jack Money" by the locals who are not profiting so well from the war industry. Part of the attraction of the Schier museum is a collection of wooden stereoscopic viewing devices that can be used to view a collection of horrific war photography. Major Holt says these photographs are a *must* —"The true horror of war: dead horses, bodies in trees, heads and legs in trenches and everywhere mud, mud, mud." O'Shea calls them war porn and finds the act of pouring over these photographs repulsive. A clear choice exists here. We did not look at them, either, but I suspect that if I go back again to the Western Front, I will have to.

Not far away is Hill 60, once the most visited place on the Flanders Front. It was actually not a natural hill at all but a mound created from the rubble from a nearby railway cutting. Now, the trenches that for years were sandbagged have filled in and one walks around a series of grass-filled cavities and mounds and memorials. The facts are there to be read and understood, but little is left to feed the visual imagination. A prolonged tunnel warfare took place at Hill 60 from February 1915 onwards, and many of the men who died there are still there under the ground. It is a mere 60 meters above sea level but classifies as a hill in "le plat pays."

In 1992, some five kilometers from the centre of Ypres, a section of trench was discovered by chance. Called the Yorkshire Trench, some 70 meters of it have been restored and preserved. We took the straight and rather characterless road from Poelkapelle to Langemark to visit it. In O'Shea's book we had read that in 1914 the trench was on both sides of this road. The German general staff sent thousands of untrained, young student volunteers to these fields when the planned Race to the Sea was misfiring, only to die in a "Massacre of the Innocents." Marching into battle as though they were on Sunday hiking outings, singing with linked arms, they were mowed down by British machine gunners. The Germans called it Der Kindermord von Ypern, and in Langemarck, a Germany cemetery contains over 44,000 bodies, many in mass graves. The Yorkshire Trench is incongruously in the middle of an industrial development that is easy to drive past. Reaching the next crossroad, we realized we had done just that and turned back. New duckboards have been put down for one to walk the length of the trench and peer down into the two dugouts that are full of water. The surrounding sheds and industrial buildings militate against any real atmosphere, and we saw no sign of any other visitors. One can do little but read the information boards and take in the fact that in this sector a new kind of duckboard was designed that made walking down the trenches marginally less unpleasant for the poor, bloody infantry who occupied them.

The city of Ypres itself was totally destroyed during the war, but never fell to the Germans. Winston Churchill famously said of Ypres that "a more sacred place for the British race does not exist in the world," and he wanted the town to be left in ruins as an eternal monument to the million men who fought in the Salient. The people of Flanders, however, had other ideas and recreated the city and its famous Cloth Hall in the city centre. The Cloth Hall houses the war museum and, as one enters, one hears the voice of the folk singer June Tabor. "Will ye go to Flanders my man?" she sings, and one walks through the rooms to the sound of voices and music. J.McCrae's *In Flanders Field* and Wilfred Owen's *Dulce et Decorum Est* are mixed with recordings that recreate the verbal testimony, in Flemish, English, German and French, from men and women who were there. This serves no celebration of glory or sacrifice, no sentimental patriotism, simply a threnody for wasted lives. McRae's poem was written in 1915, Owen's in late 1917. The change of tone is dramatic. In McCrae's poem the dead "saw sunset glow" and "lie in Flander's field," and they implore us to "take up our quarrel with the foe," which critics have since condemned as a deplorable jingoism. But two years later the fields had become a sea of filthy, stinking mud, and Owen sees a man drowning, "the white eyes writhing in his face," with "froth corrupted lungs." The sentimentality of Rupert Brooke and John McCrae is no longer acceptable, and yet McCrae's poem has, as O'Shea points out, a staying power along with other First World War clichés like "It's a Long Way To Tipperary" and "Over There."

That evening we did what all visitors to Ypres do. We went to the Menin gate where at eight o'clock every night the Last Post is played. Often, as Stephen O'Shea found when he was there, only a few curious people come, but on this particular September evening, a large crowd gathered. Moving amongst them was a group of Englishmen, all dressed in the same green blazers. They were a male voice choir from Sheffield, and they were part of what turned out to be a ceremony of some proportion. Speeches were made by various town worthies, the choir sang *Silent Night, Holy Night* and the English national anthem. Along with the Belgian trumpeters was a tall, grizzled, old kilted Scotsman playing the bagpipes to provide a drone accompaniment to the buglers of the Last Post. It was impossible not to be moved to tears by the moment, despite a feeling of guilt at what might be simply a personal indulgence. One's eyes turned up to the thousands more names of the missing inscribed on every surface of the memorial gateway: fifty-five thousand of them, regiment by regiment, British and South African and among them, as

O'Shea noted, the names of men from regiments raised in India. Everywhere in Flanders and Picardy these lists of the fallen are seen, ending sometimes with the word *Addenda* carved followed by a few extra names that somehow or other had not been included in the original count.

If one place exists where it becomes almost easy actually to visualize the Western Front as it was, that place is Newfoundland Park on the Somme where, on 1 July 1916, the First Battalion of the Royal Newfoundland Regiment went into action and, in less than half an hour, suffered what was probably the highest casualty count on that terrible day. The land was bought by the then government of Newfoundland, an area of over eighty acres with many preserved trench lines through which it is possible to walk. In other sectors, where only a small section of trench or crater has been preserved, often with its nearby cemetery of French or Belgian, British or Canadian, Australian or New Zealanders, it is not easy to do more than take in the depressing facts. Here, in this large memorial ground, the mind's eye can easily dissolve out the memorials—the Caribou emblem of the Newfoundland Regiment and the kilted Highlander of the Scottish 51st Division—and visualize the sandbags, the wire, the mud, the blasted trees, perhaps even the ghosts of the men who fought and died on the Somme whom we have seen so often in still photographs and silent films, in museums and television documentaries.

Suddenly one felt suffocated by lists. Lists everywhere,

on memorials, names, names and more names of so many nationalities. Thiepval, the largest British War memorial in the world, has even more names than the Menin Gate, over 73,000 of them under the simple bald inscription *The Missing of the Somme,* which was taken for the title of Geoff Dyer's remarkable book about the war. Thiepval stands as the prime example of what O'Shea calls "a mix of accountancy exactitude and the notion of universal victimhood." The British, he writes, invented the twentieth-century response to war. "Determine the correct tally of the dead, etch their names in stone, and avoid the sticky question of responsibility by implying that such a regrettable calamity occurred independently of human agency." So today, along with the tourist parties and their paid guides, groups of carefree school children are ushered by their harassed-looking teachers through the well laid out museum and across the carefully tended paths to the gigantic red brick memorial designed by Sir Edwin Lutyens. Many of the children laugh and giggle. How much they relate to the history around them, how much it affects them, is far from clear.

The front line at the time of the first battle of Ypres cut through the village of Zandvoorde to the south east, where the family of the singer song-writer Jacques Brel had lived. As great fans of Brel, and being so close, we could not resist a visit there. We stopped in the centre of the village and asked a morose-looking local if he could direct us to the family house. He stared at us for a moment.

Was he being militantly Flemish and showing a quiet disdain for the French language? I wondered. Then he gestured behind him. We were actually right in front of the Brel house, and a small plaque on the front wall confirmed the fact. Then he gestured to his right and indicated the memorial to Brel that stood there on the pavement. The small stone structure had carved on it the words of Brel's song about his homeland, "Le Plat Pays," in Flemish, not in the French. Although Brel did not sing directly about the War (the nearest he got to it was perhaps his song *Pourquoi ont ils tué Jaurez?*), the statue reminds us that Belgian soldiers fought this war, too, and so much of the worst of it was in their own country. When Brel sings that "it is mine," he echoes the iron will of the people who came back to Flanders and Picardy, determined to reclaim the flat country, to rebuild the ruined cities and villages and plough the fields again.

A Horse Called Humphrey

A troop of horsemen ride out of an oasis into the North African desert and disappear over the dunes to descend to the shores of the ocean. They are led by a horse master in flowing robes. He is called Achmet, but his real name is Nigel Hawthorne, and the North African desert is really a place called Patara in Southern Turkey. We were shooting a feature film, another assignment which I had been offered by HTV. It was based on a best-selling American children's novel about the first Arab horse brought to England in the early eighteenth century. It became known as the Godolphin Arabian after it passed into the possession of the Earl of Godolphin and was the progenitor of a long line of famous Arabian race horses. The story of the Godolphin Arabian is a fascinating one. Not everything is known about what happened to him between the time he was presented to the young French King Louis by the Bey of Tunis and when he was bought from a carter in the streets of Paris by an English horse trainer, played in the film by the redoubtable Frank Finlay. The book, *King of the Wind*, was a sentimental story, combining fact and fiction, about a mute Arab boy who looked after the horse and loved him dearly. Somehow or other the two of them survived a picaresque series of adventures to see the son of his horse win the Newmarket Gold Cup race in the presence of George II and his Queen Caroline. This was a co-production between HTV and an independent American film producer who had bought the rights to the book. A screenplay was credited to a writer whose name could not be found in any list of American screenwriters that I knew of. It seemed to be written by somebody who had majored in writing bubbles for comic strip books. Clearly something had to be done about that before I was besieged by a series of talented British actors waving their scripts despairingly in my face, so once again it was rewrite time, patching up dialogue into some sort of shape. Many characters in the story appeared in a small number of scenes that would require each actor to be available for only a few days of filming, which made it financially possible to have a large starry cast list. We started filming in Istanbul, to which I was no stranger having previously shot *Some Other Spring* there, as well as much earlier a TV commercial for Esso petrol, and once again I filmed in the Topkapi palace as well as other locations around the city.

For the Bey of Tunis, I was lucky to get the distinguished Shakespearean actor Ian Richardson, who brought his own imperious style and dignity to the role. The Arab lad was played by Navin Chowdhry, who had been good as the young pianist in John Schlesinger's film with Shirley MacLaine, *Madame Sousatzka*. Although he was not a pianist, he had given a very convincing performance at the keyboard. When I first met him, I mentioned the remark made by Georgie Auld the great jazz tenor saxophonist, about Robert De Niro whom he had taught to play the sax convincingly for *New York, New York*. Auld said De Niro was a bit of a pain in the arse because in his extraordinary commitment to his role as a musician, he would ring him up at all sorts of odd hours of the night with some technical question or other. I said jokingly to Naveen that I hoped he was not a pain in the arse, too, and he assured me that he certainly wasn't. In the event, he proved to be a pleasure to work with. His role was in many ways thankless because he had to play a mute boy and express all his emotions through sign language and facial expressions. He managed to do this without becoming the least bit hammy.

At one point in the story, Sham the horse was given as a gift to King Louis of France and was taken on board a ship to cross to France accompanied by Nigel and Naveen. An impressive shipbuilder was brought over to Istanbul from England to convert a local vessel, a kind of Turkish dhow, into a European schooner, which he did with impressive speed and artistry. The crew of this vessel turns out to be a rather piratical lot led by Peter Vaughan in creepy villain mode. Peter turned up on set in costume looking rather like Long John Silver. My friend Ralph Bates, whom I had cast as a French diplomat, and I walked over to admire his outfit. "Great!" I said. "What colour do you think we should have the parrot, Ralph?" The expression of horror on Peter's face as we pretended to discuss seriously this aesthetic problem was a joy to behold. When we started to laugh and he realized that we were only kidding, he told us why he had looked so apprehensive. He had played Long John Silver in a television adaptation of *Treasure Island*, and the parrot supplied for him had persisted in taking pecks at his ear. The only solution Peter could find was, just before the take, to take the poor parrot by his feet, swing him around a little so that he was dazed, and then slap him back on his shoulder in order to deliver the lines without danger of having his ear lobe bitten off.

One of the hard facts about the film industry is that if a film comes in on schedule, the production manager and associate producer go off smelling as sweet as a rose. But if, as a result of cutting corners, a film is a failure, the critics slaughter the director, not the faceless production manager. After a couple of days filming under some difficulty on the ship, we were in danger of getting behind through no fault of our own. The possibility of that happening brought forth from a lumbering and sometimes unhelpful production manager the extraordinary observation that we were shooting a tight schedule, not a movie. I corrected him with some acidity, pointing out that we were shooting a film, not a schedule, on a ridiculously tight schedule at that.

All Ian Richardson's scenes were shot in Istanbul, so we had to say thanks and good-bye to him there when we moved off to our next location in the south of Asia Minor, where we were based in a small tourist village called Kalkan. This was near the remarkable Patara Beach, a seven-mile long strand of pure golden sand bordered by a soft, gentle surf totally free of holiday makers. The beauty of the location was that the sand extended into a desert-like area behind the beach over sand dunes and, because of its position, was relatively cool to work in despite the hot sun above us. On the first day we shot there, a mile or so down the beach, we found one solitary German tourist, stark naked, enjoying his sunbathing privacy. One can imagine his dismay when he saw our caravanserai of trucks, horses and a helicopter arriving to set up our base and destroying his peaceful idyll. He hurriedly collected up his clothes and beach towel and retreated in anger. One could see his point.

Nigel Hawthorne, playing the horse master who befriends the lad, enjoyed himself hugely on the movie and said that for the pleasure of riding across the desert on his horse, he would have done the film for nothing. His horse was a grey piebald, and Nigel christened him Humphrey after his hugely successful role as the devious civil servant of that name in *Yes, Minister.* He became fond of Hum-

With Nigel Hawthorne on Patara Beach.

phrey and even thought of buying him to take him home to England but, fortunately for Nigel, the owner refused to sell, which saved him a great deal of trouble.

Nigel was a most gentle character. He loved flowers and plants, and I remember walking with him in a public garden in Turkey on one of our days off, listening to him talk knowledgeably and enthusiastically about the plants and shrubs we saw there. In the story, the horse master dies on the ship, having been beaten up by the pirates. We shot the death scene in a studio in Bristol shortly after returning to England, and that was Nigel's last scene in the film. He was immensely popular with all the crew,

Navin Choudry and Nigel Hawthorne on Humphrey

and we were sorry to say good-bye to him. After the end of filming, I received a present from him. It was a book and, knowing of my interest in jazz, he had chosen it with some thought—a biography of the great tenor saxophonist, Dexter Gordon. Nigel had written a charming and flattering inscription on the title page. I still treasure it. Not long after *King of the Wind*, Nigel made his hugely successful film of *The Madness of King George III* based on his brilliant stage performance in the role. His death from cancer was, of course, mourned by everybody, not only the theatrical community: the whole of England seemed to have taken him to their hearts. Perhaps because of *Yes, Minister* and *Yes, Prime Minister* on television, more people remembered him as Sir Humphrey than for any of his many other distinguished performances. I shall always remember Nigel, dressed in Arab costume, enjoying himself like a schoolboy riding the horse he christened with the name that had made him famous.

Ralph Bates also died sadly young from the same disease not that long after. I visited him in hospital in Hammersmith, not realizing that his cancer was terminal. Ralph, who was related to Marie Curie through his mother, probably knew he was dying, but he did not show it when I visited him.

Back in England, we filmed in and around Bath and the home of the Duke of Beaufort, which stood in for scenes in Paris and the palace of the King of France. More actors joined the cast, Frank Finlay with Jenny Agutter as his daughter, another old friend Barry Foster as a roguish inn keeper who briefly owns the horse, Jill Gascoine as his wife, and Anthony Quayle who gave a lovely and inventive cameo performance as a jovial old aristocrat, Lord Granville.

The climax of the film was the Newmarket race scene where the son of Sham wins the Gold Cup. Richard Harris and Glenda Jackson turned up to play King George II and his Queen Caroline. Although hardly major roles for either of them, Richard was well rewarded financially for his presence, and this was one of Glenda's last roles before she took up politics and became a Labour M.P. and Junior Minister. Harris and Jackson behaved like true professionals, put on their costumes and delivered their lines immac-

Frank Finlay and Jenny Agutter.

ulately, with little I could do except point the camera at them. Because they had no depth of character or motivation for me to discuss with them, this was a matter of take the money and run for the actors. I cannot forgive Richard, however, for his somewhat cynical response to questions from the press who turned up to interview the stars. It had always seemed to me that if you committed yourself to a production, then you should suspend any disbelief, and that applied as much to your views expressed publicly as to your professional behaviour. *King of the Wind* was a children's film, but I tried not to speak down to its potential audience and to apply the same standards that I would give to an adult picture. This is possibly why some critics were dismissive of the film—one American called it a total waste of time—because they could not see that it was not intended for an adult audience in the first place.

To Russia with Doubts

S̲ome time in the early nineties, my agent sent me to the Savoy Hotel to talk with a group of Italian film makers. They were in London looking for a director for an epic cinema and television movie they were going to film in the USSR based on the life of the Mongol warrior and chieftain, Genghis Khan. I was approached because of *The Far Pavilions*, which they had seen on Italian television and believed made me a suitable candidate for their project. It all sounded a bit dodgy to me from the start, and after I left a rather inconclusive meeting I forgot about the whole episode, which I had decided in my own mind was really a nonstarter.

I was taken by surprise when, some months later, the Italians opened up the dialogue again. The production company was called ICC (Italian Cinema Corporation) with offices in Rome. Despite a number of misgivings (which in the end proved to be right), I felt I had to accept the project. The challenge of shooting in the Soviet Union, which I had never visited, was irresistible, and besides, my divorce had completely cleaned me out so that I desperately needed the money. The deal was finalized after my agent, Richard Hatton, and I made one or two trips to Rome, and what turned out to be, in many ways, a bizarre experience became a reality.

A Russian director who had been involved in the project had shot some test material, but he had been paid off, rather handsomely it appeared, and although I never found out what had really happened, I got the idea that his original employment had been some sort of political move in order to get a foothold in Russia in the first place. Like many other things associated with this production, the situation was shrouded in mystery. I discovered the producers had never actually been to the location but had left all the planning to hired hands, some of whom were good. It turned out that, in fact, ICC already had an Italian film unit of about 70 technicians working in the Republic of Khirgizia where the film was to be shot: construction people, set builders, art department, costume designers and wardrobe.

This was not a good start, but I could only hope that decisions would not have been taken with which I would profoundly disagree. What did I know about Genghis Khan at that point? Not much. I read through a pile of stodgy scripts that I was sent. They covered the life of Genghis Khan, the vast Empire he created, and his astonishing military conquests that covered a large part of the known world. Already a couple of not undistinguished films about Khan had been produced. One of them starred John Wayne, which remained in my memory only as a shot of Mrs. Genghis storming back into their tent in a fury while Genghis Wayne observed that she was beautiful in her "wrath." A later one was made with Telly Savalas, James Mason and dear Michael Hordern among others, but I did not think that they were going to be much help, so I went back to the London Library to find largely out-of-print books on Genghis. The original sources were apparently a saga-like *Secret History of the Mongols* and various works by contemporary historians both Arab and European. Among the latter, according to the *Encyclopedia Britannica*, was a thirteenth century chronicler named Matthew Paris who called the Mongols "a detestable nation of Satan." The story of how a boy named Temujin became Mongol leader Genghis Khan, ruthlessly exterminating all opposition to unite the warring nomadic tribes into one nation and create the greatest continental empire of medieval times, made fascinating reading. Nevertheless, however brilliant Genghis was as a military leader, his was a nasty story of conquest based on fear, mass slaughter, torture and rapine. Many of his political strategies were designed to destroy tribal loyalties and all possibilities of internal conflict by clever dispersal of communities. Sometimes he killed all the people in a community above a certain height—the height of a cart axle—so that the children would grow up ignorant of their past to become his loyal subjects. The Mongols struck terror into the hearts of all the races they conquered. Also, they were smelly, and their odor usually preceded the advance of their all-conquering armies. It would not be easy to handle the subject and balance the exotic and romantic fascination of the story of a truly remarkable figure with the unpalatable facts of history.

To fly to Khirgizia one went via Moscow on international airlines, then on a local plane for the rest of the journey. The film company hired planes for this part of the trip which passed pleasantly enough, with caviar and Georgian champagne in plentiful supply. On my first visit to the location, I had flown from London and had several hours to spend in Moscow before joining the Roman contingent at the airport to continue the journey on to Khirghizia. In the company of a young student who had been hired for the job, I was able to make a lightning tour of the Soviet capital that I had not visited before. By this time, the early nineties, Western capitalism had already made its mark on the Russian economy. GOM, the famous department store near to Red Square, was now ablaze with adverts for Nike, Adidas, Levis and expensive perfumes. On Red Square itself, on the opposite side to Lenin's tomb and the platform above it, on which Stalin and his successors had watched the May Day Parades, was a Christian Dior Shop. That must have made the old boy turn in his tomb!

Frunze, the capital city of Khirgizia (now renamed Bishbek) was built on a grid pattern. The long streets and tree-lined avenues were oddly free of traffic except in the market area. I saw few shops, and they did not seem to be in anything resembling a city centre. No shopping precincts existed of the kind so beloved of the Western urban dweller. Until recently, a guidebook had told me, the Khirghizians were a mainly nomadic shepherd people with no experience of separate relations with the outside world. The winters there are long, hard and cold. But as an agricultural state, a plentiful supply of vegetables is available for most of the year. The roadsides near the airport were piled high with melons for sale to passing traffic.

The company had taken over a hotel completely, and the Italian crew was well settled in by the time I arrived on the scene. A number of them had formed liaisons with local girls who were now able to parade their charms in nylons and stylish Italian dresses. What stories about their marital status had been offered by the crew I do not know, but when filming stopped, as it did several weeks later, and the carpenters and electricians and set builders returned home, I suspect a number of sadly disillusioned young Russian women were left behind.

Once at the hotel I met the rest of the technicians, and the following morning we started out on my first location recce. A noisy helicopter flew us about, an old Aeroflot model, in orange paint. Inside were uncomfortable metal seats along the side of the fuselage facing inwards so that we had to sit sideways and uncomfortably to look out of the scratched windows. The engine noise was loud and overpowering, making any kind of conversation difficult. To communicate with fellow passengers, we had to shout. Most of the time it was advisable to wear a pair of ear protectors for comfort. The pilot was a Russian who spoke some English and took his instructions from an Italian who was in the co-pilot's seat beside him.

The chopper thrashed its way through the thin air above the steppes, its blades sounding like giant razors being stropped, and the steppes below us struck me as exciting and beautiful. From time to time the noise of the chopper disturbed herds of wild horses, and they would gallop away beneath us, their lovely manes flying in the wind. We landed where Marco, the production designer, had already built a Mongol township for early scenes. It was a compound of tents known as *yurts* in which the Mongol tribes lived and in which many people in the area still live today, although we were many miles from Mongolia itself.

The early part of the series covered the childhood of Genghis Khan and, returning to London, I had to cast a number of children, including the young Genghis and his friend Temujin, and adult actors as well. At the beginning, I was assured that Christopher Reeve, with whom I had worked briefly on *Superman* (and who sadly died while I was writing this book), would be playing Genghis Khan. To play him as a boy I chose a young English actor who I thought had a good resemblance to Christopher. This was Guy Faulkner, and I cast his own father James to play the role of Genghis' dad in the film. Jenny Stoller played one of his wives. In the event, Christopher Reeve was not signed up and the one American actor who eventually turned up was Lois Chiles, who played Genghis' actual mother. I got Constantin Gregory (who was Russian by birth) to act as dialogue director for the local talent that we might employ. Constantin had played a corrupt Russian officer in *Inside Out,* and he had appeared in several other films of mine including *The Waterfall.* He had worked in Moscow before on the film of John Le Carre's novel, *The Russia House,* starring Sean Connery, and had fallen in love with a Russian girl whom he subsequently married and brought back to England. I also cast him as the villainous tribal chieftain who enslaved Genghis Khan in his youth. When I considered the scripts I was given, I felt a bit like the Irishman who, when asked how to get to Limerick, answered that he wouldn't start from where the asker was in the first place. But it was too late to start again, so I insisted on having an English writer with me to get some decent shape into the scripts. I was joined by another old friend, Paul Mayersberg, who included in his credits such films as *The Man Who Fell to Earth*, which he wrote for Nic Roeg.

While Paul sat in his room struggling to give some decent shape to the script, I was involved in casting local talent. The production manager, a large amiable fellow named Piero Amati, had implored me to start shooting by a certain date, even though I did not feel prepared to do so. He said it did not matter. If I was unhappy with the material, I could always reshoot it. For reasons that never became clear to me, it was absolutely imperative that I start on the date named. Piero was also responsible for another ambitious production planned by ICC about the life of the Mongol warrior Tamberlaine, which was to be shot some time later in Samarkand, and so he flitted between the two locations. A representative of the company carrying lots of money with him had been shot in Samarkand, and ever after Piero had a police escort with him, who dined with us in the hotel restaurant. Funds arrived by courier from Rome at irregular intervals but usually accompanied by a generous supply of Pinot Grigio to keep us all happy.

From the beginning I had a deep feeling of unease about the production. Something was very odd about it. A second unit director, who seemed to have more authority than I found acceptable, was assigned to the production. For one thing, he was the company's intermediary with American talent agencies. It then transpired that he expected to direct the action scenes in the movie. I certainly did not accept that and let him know that such shooting as he did on the sequences would be under my command, which clearly did not please him at all. My assistant director, Tony Brandt, was a tower of strength. He had worked on many big productions in Rome, and we discovered that we were both avid jazz aficionados, which made a special bond between us.

I was also far from happy with the cinematographer, a Yugoslav who had moved to Western Europe and made some films in Italy. The Italians recommended him, and I can blame myself for accepting him instead of insisting on having somebody of my own choice.

Filming was agonizingly slow. One of the great problems was that truck drivers and other local technicians and supporting players lived in various villages and places around Frunze, so any last minute changes to shooting became a nightmare because of faulty lines of communication. Every morning the rackety old Russian helicopter took me, the camera crew and leading actors out to the location where we would sit around for ages in an agony of frustration, waiting for various trucks of lighting equipment and whatever to turn up so that we could begin shooting. This often did not begin until late in the morning, and one was completely powerless to do anything about it. We staggered on this way for several weeks. Rushes came back from Rome where they were being processed, and they did not look too bad. The producers pronounced themselves satisfied although surprisingly neither of the two principal company directors turned up on location. However, a charming Italian count was with us who seemed to represent the finance guarantor company.

Early in the story Genghis' father had been attacked

by another tribe of Mongols known as the Merkits. One memorably comic moment occurred with Nigel Terry, who played the wise man of the tribe. I set up a scene at the camp of Genghis' tribe where the seer galloped up from a distance through the fortified gates and jumped off his horse with the news that "The Merkits are coming!" or words to that effect. It was a long held shot on camera and required a fair bit of horsemanship from Nigel, as he had to hit a mark and jump down off his horse to deliver the line. After a couple of takes, Nigel managed it superbly. The only problem was, he got the line wrong and gasped out, "The Kermits are coming!" We all collapsed with laughter, to Nigel's astonishment as he had not realized that he had blown the line. Mercifully, he got it right on the next take.

Then Lois, our American actress, decided to quit. She had been unhappy from the start. Her costumes did not suit her, the hotel conditions were not to her satisfaction and this part of the Eastern Soviet Union was clearly not her scene at all. Neither was she particularly happy with her role. She got on a plane for home leaving me a charming note of apology. We were also approaching the end of the work permit time for the English kids, and I had not been able to shoot all the scenes with them that I needed. One morning the Italian count arrived on location with some really worrying news. In an attempted putsch by hard-line Communists, President Gorbachev had been kidnapped. It looked serious for us. If things got really bad, how would we get out? Would we be able to get a plane back to Moscow and, if not, what? Across the mountains that formed our Eastern skyline was China, and that did not seem a practical proposition. The following twenty-four hours were fraught. That evening a subdued crew sat at dinner in the hotel in an agony of uncertainty.

In my room I had a television set that normally, knowing no Russian, I did not bother to look at, but this seemed a time to at least see if one could glean any sort of intelligence from the news programmes. So I went upstairs and switched it on. Flipping the stations, I could not find any news items, but suddenly I was confronted with some alarming close-ups of sexual activity, the like of which one would certainly never see on English television and which one hardly expected to find on the box in the Soviet Union of all places. Was it being transmitted to take the public's mind off the really serious happenings in the Crimea holiday resort where Gorby was being held? Hardly likely, I thought. Then, after a flash of white, the camera backed off a little from the obscenities it was recording, and the white clearly became a toga. I was watching a Roman orgy. Then came a long shot of various chaps arriving on the scene, presumably to join the happy orgiasts. Among them was Malcolm McDowell who said something appropriate like "I don't know what is happening," but now I did. I was watching the unexpurgated version of the notorious Italian porno movie *Caligula*, with all the sequences that the director Tinto Brass had shot with hard-core porn actors from the States and added to the film after the real actors had finished their roles. Then suddenly the screen went blank.

When I reported this extraordinary event back in the hotel restaurant, nobody would believe me. I suppose I could go down in the *Guinness Book of Records* as the only Englishman at that time to have seen hard-core pornography on Soviet television. Whether or not it was a real transmission or a close-circuit one in the hotel, I was never to find out, although, as it suddenly went off air, probably somebody was getting his knuckles rapped somewhere, for it was the sort of transgression that in earlier, more repressive times might have meant a lengthy sojourn in a Siberian gulag.

The combination of the political situation and the legal obligation to return all the young actors to England meant that shooting came to a standstill. Paul's contract had expired, and he had returned to England before I left Frunze. In fact, he passed through Moscow on the historic day that Yeltsin stood on the tanks outside the Moscow Parliament building and defeated the counter-reformists. Our only option was to shut down the production for the time being and return to Rome, where I spent the next six months rewriting the script and waiting for some executive decision about the continuation of shooting. I was set up in an apartment in the Residenza di Ripetta, a place very popular with visiting film people, and to my delight Paul Mayersberg turned up a few days later. He was in Rome to work on an assignment with an Italian director and, after working all day in our respective apartments, we would go out together for an evening meal and then take coffee and a sambucco at Rosati's on the Piazza del Populo. After a few weeks Paul returned home to England, and I was on my own again, working on the script, visiting the gym and having the odd inconclusive meeting with the producer Rispoli.

One evening, the head porter at the Ripetta said to me, "A friend of yours has come to stay—Mr. Carandini, the English actor." I said, "I don't know any actor namely Carandini." He quickly responded, "You know him, the actor who plays Dracula." Christopher Lee had registered under his Italian family name—Carandini. He's done so much extended distinguished work outside the horror genre, but people still tend to think of him as Dracula. Christopher and Gitte, his wife, were sitting in a restaurant across the road, and he told me he was in Rome to work on a film, so I had good company again for the next few weeks. Whenever he had the chance, Christopher kept disappearing off to look for rare recordings of unusual performances of great 19th-century operas that he particularly liked. He was always coming back in with another one he found somewhere or other on a CD that you couldn't get in England. Later, Christopher returned to the Indian sub-continent to play the lead in a film about the life of Jinnah, the first president of Pakistan. I saw the film at a special showing at the Barbican Theatre in London. Knowing Christopher's thoroughness, I am sure he researched the story in great depth and, without question, it is one of his finest performances. Unfortunately, the film producers seem not to have secured a distribution deal in the UK so far.

At Christmas I had a short break back in England, but I was by this time becoming unhappy with the situation in Rome. I had done all I could with the script, and it was not at all clear when production would start again or even where. Finally I suggested to the producer Rispoli that it would be a good idea if I left Rome and waited for the situation to be resolved. He was clearly relieved by my proposal, and we said good-bye to each other. As I was a tax exile for a year, I could not legally return home for more than sixty days in the year without incurring punitive tax liabilities in the U.K., so I went to Ireland where I rented a house in Kinsale in County Cork for the next three months and sat down to write a thriller that I hoped had movie potential. It then turned out that the whole Genghis Khan property was sold to another company that apparently would have no responsibility for all the debts incurred to date, and that included money owed to technicians. Later the project was re-floated with the veteran Ken Annakin directing. He got a completely new script rewritten and even took a unit to China, which was not on the cards when I was under contract. But as I could have told him, it ended in tears, and his version of the film never got completed, either. This year I saw *Mongol*, a splendid film about Genghis directed by Sergei Bodrov shot—as it should be—on real locations in Mongolia and starring real Asiatic actors.

End Credits

When I returned from Ireland, I had been out of the frame for twelve months and had nothing to show for it. I was asked to direct a number of episodes of a science fiction series called *Space Precinct* produced by Gerry Anderson, who created the legendary model animation series *Thunderbirds*. *Space Precinct* as a concept was really NYPD in space, and its star was Ted Shackelford, a lean, handsome man who had starred as one of the Ewing family in the Dallas spin-off, *Knots Landing*. Ted was backed up by a young LA actor, Rob Youngblood, and a beautiful and intelligent young British actress, Simone Bendix, who looked stunning in her police uniform. The action centered around a satellite station that orbited around a planet called Altor, and all the actors playing aliens had to perform wearing weird artificial heads that looked rather like big frogs with huge eyes. A number of the police officers who appeared regularly in the show were aliens of this species, so the poor dears never showed their real faces. On top of that, performing was extremely difficult while the actor wore this alarming-looking false head because the eyes were activated by a small internal motor. An animation specialist stood on the set and controlled the eye movement by remote radio control. The motor was not totally silent, so the poor actor could not hear his cues easily. The head was not comfortable to wear, either.

The field of television had become increasingly difficult. As independent production companies struggled to get broadcasters to accept their projects, budgets and schedules were slashed in an increasingly competitive market. The single film has become a rare event and usually happens as a vehicle for a flavor-of-the-month actor who has starred in a series—possibly about hospitals, vets or coppers—and even these tend for reasons of commercial viability to be two- or three-part stories. Sadly, a tendency now exists for the director to be seen in television as little more than a kind of traffic controller, and the writer and the stars remain the more powerful part of the equation.

The hard fact of life was that the producers were getting younger and wanted directors who were younger than themselves. The older producers, scared of getting pushed to one side, were looking for the promising young directors rather than using experienced, sage hands, particularly "difficult" ones like myself, and I had never developed a long enough relationship with any television producer to overcome this problem. I had to face the hard fact that, despite critical success, I had never made a feature film that had been particularly financially successful in the States, apart possibly from *Experience Preferred But Not Essential.* That was the moment when one or two Hollywood agents started taking a passing interest in me as a possible client, but apart from a few lunches in fashionable Hollywood restaurants, nothing much came of it. Had I gone to live in L.A, as one or two of my contemporaries did, I might have had more luck in Hollywood, but I didn't for all sorts of personal and family reasons. I've never liked selling myself commercially, but at that time had I been married to my present wife Rosslyn—a PR and marketing professional who would have taken it upon herself to support and promote me—it might have been a different story. I also didn't like the scene that much. As Dorothy Parker or some other wit said, "The trouble with L.A. is that there is no there there," and I think that by this time I liked living in my own country too much to want to give up my roots. One friend of mine, Brian Eatwell, a production designer had followed the work to Hollywood but after several years came home to England. Then because of the work situation he was forced to go back to Hollywood again, because that is where the action is. Some distinguished names in the business have fallen on difficult times. Roy Boulting ended his days hard up, in a council flat in Oxford. In his later years, Michael Powell could not get any work, and on a visit to Hollywood, I gather, he had to use a public telephone on the street to make business calls. I have to be thankful, though, that I have managed to shore up a few fragments against my ruin, and that is largely due to my dear wife Rosslyn, who has looked after our finances. They say "those who can't do teach," and so I found teaching my trade to young would-be film makers an alternative. I took up teaching at a place called The London International Film School which operated out of a converted banana warehouse in Convent Garden. Students came from all over the world and, with the school director, I took part in interviews with these aspiring film makers. I am afraid that the history of cinema before Tarantino seemed a closed book to many of them and even if they had heard of *Citizen Kane*, few of them had actually seen it. Nevertheless, the really talented students were a rewarding experience and I hope that when they left the school, they took away something of value from the time I spent with them.

Two weeks before the terrorist destruction of the World Trade Center in New York, we had a fire in our house in Somerset, a much smaller disaster, of course, but one that concentrated the mind wonderfully, as the great Samuel Johnson said of a man waiting to be hanged. It nearly meant my checking in at the great film studio in the sky, but I managed to survive what was a traumatic experience for both of us.

It happened around mid-morning. Ros was out visiting her elderly mother, and I was pottering about outside when a neighbor, Paul Ketterer, pointed out that smoke was coming from an upstairs window. I rushed up to our bedroom to find the curtains in flames, made some ineffectual attempts to douse the fire with buckets of water and, after ringing the Fire Brigade, tried the garden hose through the open window. Paul's wife, Jean, also phoned the fire brigade, and he then asked me if the bedroom door was closed. Knowing I hadn't closed it, and fearing that if the fire got to the row of bookcases outside the bedroom door in the corridor the whole house might go up, I ran back upstairs to find the corridor to our bedroom full of thick black smoke. Like an idiot, I ran down the corridor, closed the bedroom door, turned back and then became completely disorientated because I could not see an inch in front of my nose. I must have passed out in seconds, and the next I knew, I was lying on a stretcher in an Air Ambulance chopper that had landed in the field behind our house. I had an oxygen mask on my face and paramedics were doing whatever paramedics do to revive somebody with serious carbon monoxide poisoning, calling my name to see if I was compos and so forth. In fact, they and the firemen were absolutely fantastic and they certainly saved my life.

Ros arrived back at the house just before they flew me off to hospital at Dorchester, and I was able to assure her that our dogs were safe, which was apparently the only thing I said to anyone! I have no recollection of that or the flight, though, and at Dorchester they found I had twenty-five percent carbon monoxide in my bloodstream, which is more than a little dangerous when, in urban high pollution areas, one percent is considered rather alarming. Then they took me by ambulance to Poole where they have a hyperbaric chamber for treating divers with the bends. I spent four deadly boring hours inside the thing with an oxygen mask on my face and a chap sitting beside me reading paperback thrillers. It was like being in a bloody submarine. "We are going down to eighteen meters," he would say as he fiddled with various controls.

I finally got a much-needed shower and a bed in the hospital around one in the morning after several hours waiting in the emergency department, where if they could think of nothing better to do with me, they would give me yet another ECG (at least I know that my heart is in good nick, which is apparently why I survived). Another two hours in the yellow submarine next morning and then Robert Shearer, a close friend in our village, collected me and took me back to Winsham.

The house was now uninhabitable, and so we stayed for the next two weeks at the home of Robert and his wife Shaune down the lane from us, before moving into temporary accommodation at a nearby farm that has holiday letting apartments. The fire was actually contained to the upstairs floor and the roof timbers, possibly because of my foolhardy efforts, but all our bedroom furniture was incinerated or soaked with water, the shower room was destroyed and a great deal of smoke and water had damaged the top floor. Many books were damaged, some ir-retrievably. Fortunately, although water came through the living room ceiling and wrecked the carpets, somehow or other the bookshelves were untouched, so all the most valuable books, CDs and records survived. What caused it, you may ask? Believe it or not, it was a convex shaving mirror on a stand reflecting the low autumn sun onto the curtains or the chest of drawers. A freak cause of fire but not unknown—it happened twice to the actor Anthony Hopkins, I am told. Now everybody we know is carefully moving mirrors, glass paperweights, cut glass ashtrays and whatever out of direct sunlight!

After the furniture was moved out, the builders gut-ted much of the empty house, and you could stand in the living room and look right up through the previously-thatched roof of our 18th century home. The situation was pretty traumatic for us and for a while Ros said she never wanted to go back and live in the house again. I under-stood how she felt, but once the major repairs were done and the surveyor discussed redecoration problems with her, she felt happy again, and eventually the house looked wonderful with no evidence at all of what happened to it.

At the beginning of 2003, I got a pleasant surprise. My agent, who had succeeded in doing nothing for me for some time, rang to say that Michael York had been trying to contact me and had left his contact numbers in L.A. I got in touch with Michael, and it turned out that a British Film Festival was opening in Denver, Colorado; Michael would be attending the Festival and his choice of film to be shown was *England Made Me*. As it happened, I had recently been able to get a sparkling new print of the film to show at the annual Graham Greene Festival in Berkhamsted, the cost of which had generously been born by Bob Allen, the executive producer and original financier of the movie, and this was shipped over to Denver for the showing. Rosslyn and I went over, and they also ran *Experience Preferred*. I promised Ros that I would not get belligerent about President Bush and Iraq, but we did not actually meet anybody in Denver who seemed the least bit happy about the Iraq war. The festival organizers, Diane Beckoff and her husband Ivan, were great hosts, and we had a marvelous time in "The Mile High City," as it is called. An American academic and film historian introduced my Graham Greene film and said that, in his opinion, it was one of the most important and underrated movies about the thirties and the rise of Nazi Germany, which, of course, pleased and flattered me no end. Unfortunately, Michael was not, in the end, able to attend the event. When we returned home after five hectic days, Rosslyn, who is a highly experienced public relations executive and film publicist, agreed to become English Representative for the festival and was soon exploiting her extensive contacts to build up a list of visiting celebrities for next year's event. We invited Jack Cardiff but Nicki, his wife, felt that the journey would be too much for him. To my surprise, the organizers decided to run *England Made Me* a second time, and this time Michael was able to turn up, and we did a double act talking about the film and answering questions.

When Roy Boulting died, the obituarist in the *Guardian* wrote, not without humour, "Film directors don't retire, they just become unbankable."

What they then do is probably write their memoirs. This is more or less what happened to me.

PETER DUFFELL
Film Director and Screenwriter

B ritish Academy Award-winning director **Peter Duffell** has made films in many countries. Educated at London and Oxford Universities where he took an Honours Degree in English Language and Literature, he entered the film industry through documentaries and TV commercials.

His first feature film, *The House That Dripped Blood* (1971), is now established as a cult horror movie, starring Peter Cushing, Christopher Lee, Denholm Elliot, Joss Ackland and Jon Pertwee.

Graham Greene, notoriously dismissive of many film adaptations of his novels, rated Peter Duffell's feature *England Made Me* (1973) as one of the best films based upon his work. Duffell both co-scripted and directed, and it starred Peter Finch, Michael York and Sir Michael Horden.

In 1981 Duffell won the **BAFTA** (British Academy of Film and Television Arts) for his direction of the 1980 multi-award winning *BBC2 Playhouse* episode "**Caught on a Train,**" starring Dame Peggy Ashcroft and Michael Kitchen.

He has also scripted and directed films based on the work of other major novelists—notably Margaret Drabble and Francis King—and has written many other screen-plays for cinema and television.

Experience Preferred But Not Essential (1982), which Duffell directed for David Puttnam, was shown at the London Film Festival and at festivals in Italy and Canada. It enjoyed huge theatrical success in America where—after a rave review by Vincent Canby in *The New York Times*—it ran for six months in one New York cinema alone.

His much acclaimed 1984 six-hour television epic *The Far Pavilions,* from the best-seller novel by M.M.Kaye, was filmed in India and starred Omar Sharif, Sir John Gielgud, Christopher Lee, Ben Cross and Amy Irving.

Les Louves (Letters to an Unknown Lover), a 1986 "film noir" starring Mathilde May, Cherie Lunghi, Ralph Bates and Andrea Ferreol, was shot in France in both French and English.

Other notable theatrical films helmed by Duffell include:

> *Inside Out*, a 1975 Warner Bros. caper movie filmed in Berlin with Telly Savalas, James Mason, Robert Culp and Aldo Ray.

> *King of the Wind*, a 1990 children's adventure film shot in Turkey and the UK, with Richard Harris, Glenda Jackson, Nigel Hawthorne, Anthony Quayle and Jenny Agutter.

Amongst Duffell's TV credits as director and writer:

The Avengers (1967)

Man in a Suitcase (1967-68)

Journey to the Unknown (1969)

The Strange Report (1969)

Black Beauty (1972)

The Racing Game (1979-80)

Inspector Morse (1988)

Space Precinct (1995)

Milton Keynes UK
Ingram Content Group UK Ltd.
UKHW050001170224
437951UK00014B/688

9 781593 936122